The Evidence of Prophecy

Fulfilled Prediction as a Testimony to the Truth of Christianity

Edited by

Robert C. Newman

Professor of New Testament
Biblical Theological Seminary

Interdisciplinary Biblical Research Institute

Hatfield, Pennsylvania

The Evidence of Prophecy:
Fulfilled Prediction as a Testimony to the Truth of Christianity

Copyright 1988 by Robert C. Newman
Second printing (with corrections) 1990
Third printing (biographical updates) 1994
Fourth printing (biographical updates) 1998

Published by the Interdisciplinary Biblical Research Institute
P. O. Box 423, Hatfield, PA 19440-0423
See our website at <www.biblical.edu>

Library of Congress Catalog Number 88-82536

ISBN 0-944788-98-X

COVER: Detail from Gustave Dore, *Amos*. Design by James I. Newman.

Contents

About the Authors

Frederick A. Aston (1899-1972) was born in Russia, where he became a Christian by studying Isaiah 53. Coming to the U.S. to prepare for ministry, he graduated from Dubuque College, Princeton Seminary, and Princeton University (M.A. in oriental languages). A severe eye problem and pastoral duties prevented his completion of Ph.D. work.

John A. Bloom (1952-) is a graduate of Grinnell College, Cornell University (Ph.D. in biophysics), Biblical Seminary, and Dropsie College/Annenberg Research Center (Ph.D. in ancient Near Eastern studies). He is Associate Professor of Physics at Biola University.

Eugenie Johnston (1951-) is a graduate of Cornell University and Biblical Seminary. She has been a missionary to St. Vincent, served on the staff of Cornell University, and is now on the staff of Cambridge College in the Boston area.

Samuel H. Kellogg (1839-99) graduated from Princeton College and Seminary. He taught theology in Allahabad, India (1864-76), at Allegheny Seminary (1877-86), held two pastorates in the U.S., and served on the revision committee for the Hindi Old Testament. In addition to a Hindi grammar, Professor Kellogg authored a number of theological books.

Robert W. Manweiler (1945-) is a graduate of the University of Kansas, Cornell University (Ph.D. in physics), and Westminster Seminary. He is currently Professor of Physics at Valparaiso University.

Robert C. Newman (1941-) is a graduate of Duke University, Cornell (Ph.D. in astrophysics), Faith Seminary and Biblical Seminary, where he is currently Professor of New Testament. He is co-author of *Science Speaks* and *Genesis One and the Origin of the Earth* and a contributor to *Evidence for Faith*.

Elaine A. Phillips (1951-) is a graduate of Cornell University, Biblical Seminary, the Institute of Holy Land Studies (M.A. in Hebrew), and Dropsie College/Annenberg Research Center (Ph.D. in rabbinic studies). She is currently Associate Professor of Old Testament at Gordon College.

Perry G. Phillips (1943-) is a graduate of Beloit College, Cornell (M.S. in physics, Ph.D. in astrophysics), Biblical Seminary, and the Institute of Holy Land Studies (M.A. in Hebrew). He has taught at Ursinus College, the Institute of Holy Land Studies and Pinebrook Junior College, and is currently Quality Assurance Engineer at Boston Technology.

Calvin E. Stowe (1802-86) graduated from Bowdoin College and Andover Seminary. He taught Greek and biblical studies at Dartmouth, Lane Seminary, Bowdoin and Andover before retiring in 1864 due to poor health. Though no longer so famous as his wife Harriet Beecher, he translated, edited and authored a number of books.

Chapter 1

Introduction

In spite of frequently alleged conflicts between science and biblical Christianity, the two have this in common: *prediction* is a concept at the heart of both. As the Bible says, "Faith is being sure of what we hope for [i.e., the future] and certain of what we do not see [the invisible world]" (Heb 11:1). Similarly, scientists are impressed by theories that successfully predict and unimpressed by theories that don't.

Of course, many view religion as the very antithesis of science. Religion, they say, is superstition, a leap in the dark, believing what you know isn't true. Science, on the contrary, is rooted and grounded in evidence. A scientist should believe nothing he cannot prove.

While I cannot speak for other religions, these definitions are distortions of biblical Christianity and of science. Of course Christianity has a central place for faith: "Without faith it is impossible to please God, because anyone who comes to him must believe that he exists and that he rewards those who earnestly seek him" (Heb 11:6). But faith is central to science, also. Without believing that physical laws exist and that they will reward those who earnestly seek them, no one would ever have started the activity we call science. And without such a faith continuing, it is doubtful that science can long endure. Both science and biblical Christianity have a central place for faith commitments.

But both have a central place for evidence, too. While it is true that there is a fideistic wing of Christianity that treats evidence as a concession to sinners and makes a virtue of believing without evidence, this is a distortion of biblical Christianity. The apostle Paul expressly tells Christians to "Test everything. Hold on to the good" (1 Thess 5:21). Luke the Gospel writer says of his research into the life of Jesus, "I myself have carefully investigated everything from the beginning ... so that you may know the certainty of the things you have been taught" (Luke 1:3-4). Jesus rebukes his opponents for not using the same methods to test his claims as they use to study the weather (Matt 16:1-4; Luke 12:54-56).

Fulfilled Prophecy as Evidence

Among the evidences put forth by the Bible for the truth of biblical Christianity, fulfilled predictions are especially important. The Bible presents us with a revealed religion, explaining that we live in a universe marred by sin. As a result, we need a revelation of God's remedy for sin in order to know what we must do. Otherwise, how can we avoid the ultimate disaster of facing God's judgment with a case that won't stand up in court? Consequently, God began to send prophets early in Israel's history so that his people might know what he required and how they were doing. God's instructions for this class of spokesmen-prophets are detailed in the 18th chapter of Deuteronomy.

Not all of the prophets' messages were predictive. Most of them were intended to remind the people of God's laws for abundant living and of their foolishness in thinking they could have a better life by doing their own thing. Yet prediction was important to *verify* a prophet's credentials. The prophet's authority was in principle enormous; the Israelites were to obey whatever he said. "I will raise up for them a prophet like you from among their brothers; I will put my words in his mouth, and he will tell them everything I command him. If anyone does not listen to my words that the prophet speaks in my name, I myself will call him to account" (Deut 18:18-19). Naturally, such authority provided a strong temptation for charlatans to claim prophetic gifts. To counter this temptation, God provided a strong deterrent: conviction for false prophecy bore the death penalty. "But a prophet who presumes to speak in my name anything I have not commanded him to say ... must be put to death" (Deut 18:20).

One of the main tests for false prophecy was inaccuracy of prediction. If a prophet erred in only one prediction, he was a false prophet! "You may say to yourselves. 'How can we know when a message has not been spoken by the LORD?' If what a prophet proclaims in the name of the LORD does not take place or come true, that is a message the LORD has not spoken. That prophet has spoken presumptuously. Do not be afraid of him" (Deut 18:21-22).

As the centuries passed, claimants for the office of prophet began to show up. What may surprise many is the fact that some of these claimants passed the test. Two contests between true and false prophets are recorded in Scripture. In 1 Kings 22, Zedekiah and his associates are shown by the course of events to be false prophets in confidently predicting that Ahab king of Israel would defeat the Syrians at Ramoth Gilead. Their opponent Micaiah is vindicated in his prediction (at some risk to his own life) that Ahab will be killed. Before he is vindicated, Micaiah calls attention to this fulfillment test (v 28). In Jeremiah 28, Hananiah is shown to be a false prophet when his popular prediction fails regarding Nebuchadnezzar's defeat and the return of Judah's king and temple treasures within two years. Jeremiah is vindicated when he rejects these predictions before the fact and warns that Hananiah will die that very year.

The mechanism behind this test is quite simple. God controls the future: he supports his own prophets while defeating false ones. "I am the LORD, who has made all things ... who foils the signs of false prophets and makes fools of diviners ... who carries out the words of his servants and fulfills the predictions of his messengers" (Isa 44:25-26). As best we can tell, the written predictions of biblical prophets were made by those who passed this test.

Alternative Explanations

At this point, someone might object that the accuracy of biblical prediction is just a result of selection: only those predictions were preserved which were actually fulfilled. To this we respond: we have no way of knowing what was done centuries ago unless it was recorded. Of course, we can fantasize any reconstruction of history to avoid problems for our own worldview, but if we really want to know what happened, this is dangerous business. There is no evidence in Scripture that editors removed or refused to record disfulfillments. In fact, many predictions of the Bible were not fulfilled until centuries after the Bible was written, and it is these we will concentrate on in the course of this book.

Perhaps one might prefer the explanation that some people just naturally have an extrasensory prophetic gift. The Hebrews were merely unusual in developing a selection mechanism to locate such individuals. I would respond that this is not the Bible's explanation. It is usually safer to accept an explanation for a given ability from one who has the ability than from one who doesn't. In any case, this explanation does not handle other evidences for the truth of biblical Christianity.[1]

From a scientific perspective, man has a limited ability to predict the future which rapidly erodes as the prediction becomes more detailed or applies to more distant times. It used to be thought that in principle man could predict any event at any distance to any required level of detail, the only limitation being a sufficiently powerful computing machine. But even if Newtonian physics were true, this ideal is hopelessly optimistic. Suppose one knew the position and speed of every particle in the universe at some point in time. To calculate their subsequent movements, one's computer must have a least one element for each particle; the machine will therefore be at least as big as the universe itself. Even to keep up with the existing universe, the machine must transfer information within itself at the speed of light, since that is what light does in our universe. Apparently the optimum computing machine would be a parallel universe, but it could never get ahead of the real one due to unavoidable delays in getting the information and setting it up!

In this century discoveries in the field of quantum mechanics indicate that we (being inside the universe) have no tools by which we can exactly specify both the position and speed of even one particle, much less all of them. Thus our ability to predict the location of any one particle rapidly disintegrates as time passes, even with an infinitely large computer at our disposal.

Consequently we will suggest that the materials we examine in this book provide strong evidence that the Bible is a bona fide revelation from the God who controls history.

Plan of This Book

In the next chapter, we will consider the great contrast that exists between biblical prophets and pagan prophets, using the Greek oracles as our pagan example. The rest of the book will consider in some detail specific examples of fulfilled biblical prophecies, grouping them by subject matter into prophecies concerning the nations, prophecies about Israel, and prophecies involving the Messiah. In a final chapter we will consider the implications of our findings.

Acknowledgments

This book is an outgrowth of a seminar on fulfilled prophecy held at Biblical Theological Seminary in 1974. Papers submitted by several students in that course (chs 3, 4, 5 and 8) have been supplemented by my own work (chs 1, 9 10 and 12), plus several works of others (chs 2, 6, 7 and 11). The whole has been edited to produce a more unified style and outlook.

My thanks to former students Bob Manweiler (ch 3), Perry Phillips (ch 4), Elaine Phillips (ch 5), John Bloom (ch 7) and Eugenie Johnston (ch 8) for their good work; to Mrs. Frederick A. Aston, for permission to use an article by her late husband which for many years was issued as a pamphlet, *The Challenge of the Ages*. The material in chapter 2 has been adapted from chapter 13 of Calvin E. Stowe, *The Origin and History of the Books of the Bible* (Hartford: Hartford Publishing Co., 1867). Chapter 6 is an adaptation of the first two chapters of Samuel H. Kellogg, *The Jews, or Prediction and Fulfillment*, 2nd ed. (New York: Anson D. F. Randolph, 1887).

Thanks to Hilary and Joy Nixon for their financial aid in the initial printing of this book, and to Jim Newman for cover design and illustrations.

Chapter 2

Biblical Prophecy and Pagan Oracles

Calvin E. Stowe

So far as we know, the ancient nations all had prophets, whether or not they could really predict the future. Yet the fact that pretended prophets exist does not prove that true prophets do not. Such an argument need be no stronger than the claim that the existence of counterfeit money proves there is no genuine! Indeed, the existence of prophetic claims on such a scale might suggest the existence somewhere of true prophecy. As the existence of the eye presupposes light, may not the universal human tendency to worship imply mankind was designed to have a true object of worship? Similarly, the universal desire for communication from God may suggest it has really happened somewhere in human history.

Our concern, however, is not whether prophets existed among the pagan nations. They did. We want to know whether these prophets are like those of the Bible or whether the differences between them are such as to indicate that their abilities and messages come from different sources. The Bible repeatedly claims such a difference, one so obvious that anyone who observes both kinds of prophets has no excuse for confusing one with the other. Let us look at some evidence from antiquity to see how this is so.

Hebrew and Pagan Religions

The Hebrews were unique among the peoples of the ancient world in worshiping only one God, the creator and ruler of the universe. In order that they might continue to do so, they were instructed by Scripture and also by prophets who claimed to receive God's will by direct revelation. The prophets were to encourage obedience to God's law, to instruct the people when they were ignorant, and to warn them when they went astray. To prove the validity of their claim to speak for God, the prophets professed to predict future events beyond human foresight and to work miracles beyond human power.

The surrounding nations worshipped various gods, and they too had prophets who claimed to be inspired by these gods. These nations usually recognized the God of the Hebrews as really a God and His prophets as true prophets. The difference was that the Hebrews claimed their God and prophets were the only true ones, while the pagans merely claimed their gods were equal to Jehovah and their prophets to His prophets (1

Kings 20:28).

In many biblical passages, God rebukes the pagan nations for this error and calls on them to renounce it. In Isaiah 45, after a detailed prediction regarding king Cyrus, where he is named and his actions are described more than 150 years before he was born, the God of the Hebrews is pictured as declaring that He uttered this prediction for the very purpose of showing Cyrus that the God of Israel is the only true God.

This passage also contrasts God's creative power, his straight-forward speech, and his unfailing truthfulness with the crookedness, cunning and lies of the pagan gods (vv 18-19). He calls all nations to come together and, before them all, appeals to this prophecy as an example of foreknowledge completely beyond the reach of the heathen prophets and a proof that He alone is the true God and his prophets the only true prophets (vv 20-22).

Let us elaborate on this idea here. By contrasting Hebrew with pagan prophets, we shall seek to show that only the former have a real claim to divine inspiration.

Prophets of Ancient Greece

Of all the nations in the ancient world, the Greeks have the greatest reputation for education and civilization. The Greeks had their prophets also. To them the Greek moralists, lawgivers and magistrates submitted the most important questions. Their decisions were considered sacred and binding. Since the prophets of Greece are among the best the pagan world can furnish, they will be used for comparison with the prophets of the Bible.

So you can make the comparison for yourself, we will attempt a brief but accurate description of the Greek prophets as represented by the Greek historians and of the Hebrew prophets as represented by the Bible.[1] Thus each nation will give its own account of those for whom it claims divine inspiration and ability to predict the future.

Among the Greeks there was a class of people called *theomantes* who may in some ways be compared with the Hebrew prophets. These were a combination of travelling preacher and fortune-teller -- wandering through the country, giving advice on moral duties, chanting passages from the poets, and claiming to predict the future. Yet they would never give a prediction until an offering had been made and certain ceremonies exactly carried out, a device commonly used by charlatans to enrich themselves and distract their audience from their sleight of hand. Poorly qualified as these theomantes were to be religious teachers, they were the only source of spiritual guidance for the lower classes. As it happens, none of the teachings of the theomantes have survived to the present.

Greek Oracles

More properly compared to the Hebrew prophets are those who officiated at the various oracles. These people separated from society to some remote location, where a thick forest, high mountain, waterfall or cave might arouse awe in their clients and encourage them to believe this was the home of some pagan god. Living in such mysterious isolation, they claimed to have contact with the supernatural world. All who wished a consultation must come to them. No one could get a response to his questions until he had presented gifts and passed through various ceremonies.

These ceremonies put the client in such a state of mind as would hinder his detecting any trickery. The client then received the divine response to his question, cleverly put in verse by poets hired for the purpose. The language of the answer was carefully chosen to be more or less ambiguous and sometimes even unintelligible. Many of these oracles or prophecies have been preserved by the Greek historians.

From the responses which survive we can see what sort of questions were asked and how they were answered.[2] Religion or morality is seldom mentioned. The responses are mainly concerned with politics, warfare, migrations, and disputes between nations or individuals. When the oracles were asked to settle disputes, one party often bribed them to give a decision against the other. If the oracles wished to stay in favor with both parties, they would procrastinate or evade the question. When the outcome of some public action was demanded, the oracles sometimes consulted men with political experience to find out what answer was safe. At other times the answer was worded so that it could be interpreted to give two opposite meanings. If these devices could not be used, the oracle might refer the inquirer to astrology or magic for a decision. Or the oracle might evade the point by abuse or sarcasm. If nothing else seemed likely to work, the priests of the oracle could always say their god was angry and unwilling to answer.

What is notable in all these prophecies is that they seldom have any good moral tendency. Virtue is not rewarded, vice is not punished. The powerful are flattered, no matter how unjust they are. The weak are left unprotected, no matter how innocent. The worst idolatry is encouraged, in many cases extending to human sacrifice. A large donation was usually the only way to get an answer from the oracle.

Every part of this description of the Greek prophets can be verified by quotations from the Greek historians.[3]

Oracles of Delphi and Trophonius

Some of the most important Greek oracles owed their fame to

intoxicating gases coming up from subterranean caverns. Among the oracles of ancient Greece, none had more customers than that of Apollo at Delphi. According to Diodorus Siculus, the cave at Delphi was discovered by accident:[4]

> There is a chasm at this place where now is situated what is
> known as the "forbidden" sanctuary, and as goats had been wont
> to feed about this because Delphi had not as yet been settled,
> invariably any goat that approached the chasm and peered into
> it would leap about in an extraordinary fashion and utter a sound
> quite different from what it was formerly wont to emit. The
> herdsman in charge of the goats marvelled at the strange
> phenomenon, and having approached the chasm and peeped
> down it to discover what it was, had the same experience as the
> goats, for the goats began to act like beings possessed, and the
> goatherd also began to foretell future events.

After the oracle was established, the effect of this gas on the officiating priestess was similar. No sooner was she inspired, than she began to swell and foam at the mouth, tearing her hair, cutting her flesh, and in all her behavior appearing like one frantic and distracted. In some instances the effect was so violent as to kill the priestess immediately.

At the oracle of Trophonius, the client's contact with the oracle was more direct. Pausanius describes the procedure involved:[5]

> When a man has made up his mind to descend to the oracle
> of Trophonius, he first lodges in a certain building for an
> appointed number of days, this being sacred to the good Spirit
> and to good Fortune.

He was to purify himself by various means and to offer sacrifices to several different deities before he was ready to descend to meet the god.

> The procedure of the descent is this. First, during the night
> he is taken to the river Hercyna by two boys... who... anoint him
> with oil and wash him.... After this... he must drink water called
> the water of Forgetfulness, that he may forget all he has been
> thinking of hitherto, and afterwards he drinks of another water,
> the water of Memory, which causes him to remember what he
> sees after his descent...[6]

The oracle is in a cave, reached only by descending into a narrow artificial pit, six feet wide and twelve feet deep.

> They have made no way of descent to the bottom, but when
> a man comes to Trophonius, they bring him a narrow, light
> ladder. After going down he finds a hole between the floor and
> the structure. Its breadth appeared to be two spans [about 20"]
> and its height one span. The descender lies with his back on the
> ground, holding barley-cakes kneaded with honey, thrusts his feet
> into the hole and himself follows, trying hard to get his knees into
> the hole. After his knees the rest of his body is at once swiftly

drawn in, just as the largest and most rapid river will catch a man in its eddy and carry him under. After this those who have entered the shrine learn the future, not in one and the same way in all cases, but by sight sometimes and at other times by hearing. The return upwards is by the same mouth, the feet darting out first.[7]

The visitor was always pale and depressed on his return, so that it became proverbial to say of one who was depressed: "he has consulted the oracle of Trophonius."

It was probably in contrast to oracles such as these that the LORD declares, "I have not spoken in secret, in a dark place of the earth." In contrast with the difficulty of getting answers from an oracle, and the ambiguous and unintelligible language of the oracle when it did answer, God also says: "I said not to the seed of Jacob, seek ye me in vain. I the LORD speak righteousness, I declare things that are right." As Lowth translates it, "I speak truth and give direct answers" (Isa 45:19).

The time for consulting the Delphic oracle was originally only during one month of the year, and generally on the seventh day of the month, which was considered Apollo's birthday. Even later, when responses were given more frequently, they could never be gotten more often than once a month. And they were expensive!

Whoever went to consult the oracle was required to make large presents to the god, whereby it came to pass that this temple, in riches, splendor and magnificence, was superior to almost all others in the world.... It was the custom also to offer sacrifices to Apollo, in which except the omens were favorable, the prophetess would not give an answer. At the sacrifices there were five priests that assisted the prophets, and another priest also that assisted the prophetess in managing the oracle.[8]

As those priests were the sole judges of the omens, it was very easy for them to evade every question on which it might be dangerous for them to commit themselves.

Among the presents which Croesus, king of Lydia, sent to this oracle, Herodotus enumerates the following:[9]

He melted down a vast store of gold and made of it ingots of which the longer sides were of six and the shorter of three palms' length, and the height was one palm [1 palm = about 3 inches]. These were an hundred and seventeen in number. Four of them were of refined gold, weighing two talents and a half [1 talent = about 60 lb]; the rest were of gold with silver alloy, each of two talents' weight. He bade also to be made a figure of a lion of refined gold, weighing ten talents.... When these offerings were fully made, Croesus sent them to Delphi, with other gifts besides, namely two very great bowls, one of gold and one of silver.... The golden bowl... weighs eight talents and a half, and twelve minae... and the silver bowl... holds six hundred nine-gallon measures.... Along with these Croesus sent, besides many other offerings of no great mark... a golden female figure three cubits [4-1/2 feet] high.

Character of the Oracular Responses

The general nature of the answers given by the oracles is accurately described by the pagan Cicero:[10]

But now I come to you, "Apollo, sacred guard of earth's true core / Whence first came frenzied, wild prophetic words." Chrysippus filled a whole volume with your oracles; of these some, as I think, were false; some came true by chance, as happens very often even in ordinary speech; some were so intricate and obscure that their interpreter needs an interpreter and the oracles themselves must be referred back to the oracle; and some so equivocal that they require a dialectician to construe them. For example, when the following oracular response was made to Asia's richest king: "When Croesus o'er the river Halys goes / He will a mighty kingdom overthrow," Croesus thought he would overthrow his enemy's kingdom, whereas he overthrew his own. But in either event the oracle would have been true.

Herodotus informs us that when Croesus, after this defeat, complained to the priestess of Apollo that she had deceived him, she replied:[11]

Croesus doth not right to complain concerning it. For Loxias declared to him that if he should lead an army against the Persians he would destroy a great empire. Therefore it behoved him, if he would take the right counsel, to send and ask whether the god spoke of Croesus' or of Cyrus' empire. But he understood not that which was spoken, nor made further inquiry; wherefore now let him blame himself.

To illustrate still further the questions asked the Greek prophets and the way they handled them, we give two more examples from Herodotus:

Nor were they [the Spartans] satisfied to remain at peace; but being assured that they were stronger than the Arcadians, they inquired of the oracle at Delphi, with their minds set on the whole of Arcadia. The Pythian priestess gave them this reply: "Askest Arcadia from me? 'Tis a boon too great for the giving / Many Arcadians there are, stout heroes, eaters of acorns, / These shall hinder thee sore. Yet 'tis not I that begrudge thee: / Lands Tegean I'll give thee, to smite with feet in the dancing, / Also the fertile plain with line I'll give thee to measure." When this was brought back to the ears of the Spartans, they let the rest of the Arcadians be, and marched against the men of Tegea carrying fetters with them; for they trusted in the quibbling oracle and thought they would enslave the Tegeans. But they were worsted in the encounter, and those of them who were taken captive were made to till the Tegean plain, wearing the fetters which they themselves have brought, and measuring the land with a line.[12]

The Spartans, having been repeatedly defeated by the Tegeans, again sent to consult the Delphic oracle. The priestess told them that if they could find the bones of Orestes, they would be "a helper of Tegea." The Spartans finally found what they thought might be these bones and conquered Tegea.[13]

Both of these oracles are quite ambiguous in the original Greek. They would have been equally true whether the Spartans or Tegeans won. They also sanction glaring injustice. There is no hint to the Spartans that their planned attack on the peaceful Tegeans, to rob them of land and liberty, is against all principles of justice. Nor does the historian himself seem to think it wrong for the Spartans to make war because they were tired of peace, nor a fault in the oracle that it says nothing of moral obligation. Politics not morality, war and revenge not peace and goodwill, were the topics most acceptable to the prophets of ancient Greece.

Herodotus also gives us details of the oracles given to the Athenians on the outcome of the Persian invasion,[14] as well as several others elsewhere in his history. These are all of the same character as those described above.

It is well known that the Greek oracles were frequently bribed by politicians to give answers that would promote their own schemes. Plutarch tells us that a certain general Themistocles:

... despairing to bring the multitude over to his views by any human reasonings, set up machinery, as it were, to introduce the gods to them, as a theatrical manager would for a tragedy, and brought to bear upon them signs from heaven and oracles.[15]

Demosthenes publicly complained that the Delphic oracle, being bribed by Philip, *philipized.*[16]

Such was the reputation which the Greek oracles had with the most intelligent of the Greeks themselves. In this description of the Greek prophets, as given by the Greek historians, we find all the standard human traits of selfishness, deception and crime. How easy for these pretended prophets to deceive any time they wished to! Their whole system of operation looks very much like an attempt to conceal a profitable fraud! Most likely, the phenomena known today as hypnotism, clairvoyance and spiritism also aided in the success of the ancient oracles. Surely, as the Bible says, "they have no knowledge who carry about their wooden idol, and pray to a god who cannot save. He feeds on ashes; a deceived heart has turned him aside. And he cannot deliver himself, nor say, 'Is there not a lie in my right hand?' " (Isa 45:20; 44:20).

The Hebrew Prophets

From this scene of pagan deception and credulity, let us now turn to the prophets of the Bible. In every respect we find them the opposite of those just described. They sought no concealment and pretended to no mystery. They lived in their society more or less like other people. They were accessible to those who wished their advice, and gave it freely without asking gifts or requiring ceremonies to awe those consulting them. No techniques were employed to put on airs of sacredness, though they sometimes acted out parables to gain the attention of the people.

Their prophecies were neither evasive nor ambiguous. Instead they were prompt, direct and decisive. On all occasions of great public concern, the prophets appeared in public and taught the crowds with sincerity and passion. Frequently these pubic addresses were written down, and we have them in every form, from the simplest prose to the most lofty poetry. The writings of the Hebrew prophets which have come down to us are so extensive that we have no difficulty in learning the usual subjects and character of their prophecies.

Character of the Hebrew Prophecies

Religion was the great subject on which they loved to dwell, and with them religion was neither empty talk nor superstitious ceremony. The love and worship of one God, spiritual and holy; obedience to his law; purity of heart as the most acceptable sacrifice -- these constituted the religion of the Hebrew prophets. In contemplating such subjects their spirits rose on the wings of a holy ecstasy to the very throne of God on high, which no mortal eye but theirs had ever seen, and no mortal tongue had ever dared to celebrate.

In all their prophecies there was the constant aim to exert the best moral influence. Calamity they always threatened as the punishment of sin, and prosperity was the sure reward of holy obedience. To the corruption of their society they presented independent, bold and unyielding opposition. They fearlessly withstood ungodly rulers with severe and public rebuke. When both king and people united against the laws of God, the prophets stood forth in the face of hatred, persecution, prison and death to give direct, unequivocal and solemn declarations of God's hatred of such evil and His vengeance against it. They pointedly condemned such superstitious activities as astrology, magic and spiritism, even though these practices were popular. They rejected the rich presents which were occasionally offered them. Their predictions of future events were usually public, clear, easy to understand, and such as no human foresight could have guessed.

Illustrations from the Old Testament

Examples of the features noted above occur so frequently that one who has any acquaintance with the Old Testament will have no trouble verifying this description. Recall how Elisha refused the royal gifts of Namaan (2 Kings 5); how Isaiah publicly and severely rebuked idolatrous king Ahaz (Isa 7); how steadfastly Jeremiah resisted the rebellion of his king and nation, though their opposition wounded him so deeply that he often wished for death to put an end to his anguish. In the whole character of the Hebrew prophets we see an openness which disdained concealment and a virtue which hated deception.

The prophet Nathan did not refrain from picturing king David's adultery and murder in its true colors and boldly saying, "You are the man!" (2 Sam 12).

The prophet Elijah knew that king Ahab had been searching everywhere to arrest and execute him, but he fearlessly came to meet him at the appointed time. When the king greeted him "Is this you, you troubler of Israel?" he instantly replied, "I have not troubled Israel, but you and your father's house have, because you have forsaken the commandments of the LORD, and you have followed the Baals" (1 Kings 18).

On another occasion, when the same king had killed Naboth to get his vineyard, Elijah met him with this appalling message: "Thus says the LORD, 'In the place where the dogs licked up the blood of Naboth the dogs shall lick up your blood, even yours.' " When Ahab responded, "Have you found me, O my enemy?" Elijah answered, "I have found you, because you have sold yourself to do evil in the sight of the LORD." Where in the whole literature of the pagan oracles do we find such resistance to tyranny or defense of injured and helpless innocence, to compare with this?

Conclusions

And now isn't the difference between the Hebrew and pagan prophets obvious? In the one case we see all the machinery of fraud, a total lack of moral feeling, and every indication of an exclusive attachment to this world. In the other case we can discover no wish nor opportunity to deceive. We find an acute moral sensitivity and an inflexible adherence to what is right, and a total renunciation of all worldly hopes whenever they interfered with the call of duty. The former is just what we would expect from men of this world, who have no faith in another. The latter is just what we should expect from men of God, who have placed all their hopes in heaven. Who, with any knowledge of the subject, can place these two classes on equal ground or say they have equal claims to divine inspiration?

How can we account for the fact that the Hebrews, who were so far behind the Greeks in civilization, science and education, were so far above them in the character of their religious teachers? The Bible has the answer, given through Moses, one of the greatest Hebrew prophets:

See, I have taught you statutes and judgments just as the LORD my God commanded me, that you should do thus in the land where you are entering to possess it. So keep and do them, for that is your wisdom and your understanding in the sight of the peoples who will hear all these statutes and say, "Surely this great nation is a wise and understanding people." For what great nation is there that has a God so near to it as is the LORD our God whenever we call on Him? Or what great nation is there that has statutes and judgments as righteous as this whole law which I am setting before you today? (Deut 4:5-8).

Part One

Prophecies about the Nations

Chapter 3

The Destruction of Tyre

Robert W. Manweiler

One of the most striking examples of fulfilled prophecy in the Bible is that of Ezekiel 26 against the ancient Phoenician seaport of Tyre. Here we want to look first at some details of this prediction, then at historical records covering the time of its fulfillment. Finally we will consider the date of the passage, its integrity, and alternative explanations some have proposed to avoid accepting fulfilled prophecy.

Ezekiel is probably the most carefully dated of all Old Testament books. Postponing our discussion of its authenticity until later, we here note that the majority of biblical scholars, even of those who reject the inspiration and unity of the Bible, believe most of the book was written in the sixth century BC by the prophet Ezekiel. The prophecy against Tyre in chapter 26 can be dated with great probability at least two centuries before its fulfillment.

The historical setting of Ezekiel's Tyre prophecy is clearly set forth in the book itself. Ezekiel's prophecies are concerned with (1) the dissolution and destruction to come on Israel's southern kingdom, called Judah; (2) the destruction of various foreign nations and cities; and, by contrast, (3) God's promise of a future hope for Israel. Ezekiel dates each prophetic utterance in years since the captivity of Jehoiachin, king of Judah. King Nebuchadnezzar had carried him off to Babylon in 597 BC. Ezekiel had been taken captive also, and was called to be a prophet in the fifth year of this chronology.

Chapter 26 of Ezekiel is dated in the eleventh year, about 587 BC, shortly before Jerusalem itself was destroyed by the Babylonians. The chapter is a prophecy against the city of Tyre, stronghold of the seafaring Phoenicians. For the previous 600 years Tyre had been an important sea power. The city was located on the eastern coast of the Mediterranean, about one hundred miles north of Jerusalem. The older part of city, called Old Tyre, was on the shore. About a half mile offshore was an island, called Insular Tyre, which was also fortified and had both northern and southern harbors. Ancient references to Tyre clearly indicate both its coastal nature and its island development.[1] Pliny, for instance, says that Old Tyre was about fifteen miles in circumference, though the island was only about four miles around. The onshore city was thus the major part of the metropolis, with a population of some tens of thousands.

Ezekiel's Prophecy

Ezekiel 26 divides easily into an introduction and four distinct sections. The introduction (vv 1-3a) states that the LORD has determined to destroy Tyre because it turned against Jerusalem. In the first of the four sections (vv 3b-6), we are told that *many nations* will come against Tyre. In the second section (vv 7-11), the prophet focuses upon *one* of these many nations, Babylon, and its king, Nebuchadnezzar. Then in the third section (vv 12-14), the subject of the action shifts from singular to plural, from "he" (Nebuchadnezzar) to "they."

To whom does this pronoun "they" refer? Some feel it continues the reference to Nebuchadnezzar, changing to plural as a literary device for emphasis; others that it shifts the focus from Nebuchadnezzar to his armies. However, there are good reasons for rejecting these suggestions and identifying "they" with the "many nations" of the first section. For one thing, if these nations are not mentioned again, section one is left incomplete and dangling. In addition, several events mentioned in the first section are repeated in the third section but not the second. This makes it natural to identify the subjects of the first and third sections. Thirdly, a return to the original subject, "many nations" (or at least another example of such), not only explains the sudden shift from singular to plural, it also completes the symmetry of the prophecy. Guesses about multiple authors or editors need not be invoked. Finally, the idea that the number change is only a literary device is difficult and unnatural. We suggest that the plural verbs of the third section point to a further specific example of the general subject of section one, "many nations," the thought shifting from Nebuchadnezzar's siege against Tyre to a campaign by other nations.

The fourth and final section (vv 15-21) of the chapter is a poetic lamentation and a partial restatement of the predicted events, concentrating on the final outcome for Tyre and the reaction of surrounding nations.

Some *unusual* statements concerning what is to be accomplished by the many nations attacking Tyre are found in the first section. The dirt or debris of Tyre is to be scraped from the city, which is to be made like the surface of a rock (v 4). The prophecy does not indicate which nation or nations will accomplish this or when it will occur, but the event is none the less vivid for that. More commonplace statements of destruction also occur, like, "she will become spoil for the nations."

The feats to be accomplished by Nebuchadnezzar in the second section are typical of a successful land campaign. Horses, chariots and cavalry are used. Siege walls are built. He enters the city and dust from the cavalry covers it. People are slain. This section clearly refers to the conquest of an onshore city, like Old Tyre, as the details are not appropriate to an island assault. It is also noteworthy that the *first* section says many nations will plunder Tyre, but this is never said of Nebuchadnezzar's campaign. Thus a contradiction often alleged between v 5 of our passage and Ezek 29:18-20 (where Nebuchadnezzar's army gets no plunder from Tyre) is *not* a contradiction if v 5 is referring to plundering by another nation or nations at a different time.

The third section is also quite vivid: a nation or nations from among the "many nations" is to throw Tyre's stones, timbers and debris *into the water* (v 12). Compare this with v 4 in section one, above, and note the apparent continuity of subject. The statement is indeed most peculiar, found nowhere else in Scripture. Furthermore, the walls will be destroyed and "they" -- the many nations -- will plunder Tyre's riches and merchandise. The city will *not be rebuilt* again (vv 13, 14, 19 and 21). The people will be slaughtered and the coastlands shaken at her fall. Thus the glorious and mighty city is to be destroyed, the people broken. Since the subject of section two concerning Nebuchadnezzar precedes section three and is not to be identified with it, the sacking of Tyre is (implicitly) not attributed to Nebuchadnezzar. Section three would most naturally follow section two chronologically, and a gap in time between the two sections is not unreasonable.

The History of Tyre After the Prophecy

Let us now see what happened to Tyre since Ezekiel's time. The reference to Nebuchadnezzar in the second section of the prophecy is not surprising, since Ezekiel himself was carried away captive by this mighty Babylonian king. According to the Jewish historian Josephus,[2] Nebuchadnezzar besieged Tyre for thirteen years from 585 to 573 BC, starting shortly after the destruction of Jerusalem. Thus Nebuchadnezzar's predicted activity would have started just a year or two after the date of Ezekiel's prophecy.

From our perspective twenty-five hundred years later, we cannot independently test whether Ezekiel wrote before or after Nebuchadnezzar's siege. Thus we cannot *prove* this part was prophecy; we can only show that no contradiction with other historical sources occurs. Unlike us, however, a person living at Ezekiel's time could well know this siege was prophesied. Of course, admitting Ezekiel made such a prediction, one might object that this would require little insight at the time, when Nebuchadnezzar was conquering the whole Mediterranean coastland.

Even so, it is interesting to note the accuracy of the account extending to small details. For instance, Nebuchadnezzar evidently did not have a very successful siege. He finally broke through the walls of Old Tyre, but by then most of the Tyrians had retreated to Insular Tyre. Nebuchadnezzar was thus deprived of the opportunity to plunder their wealth and pay his army (see Ezek 29:18-20) after a siege of thirteen years! As far as we can tell, no event which Ezekiel assigns to the Babylonian king in this prophecy failed to occur.

If the Babylonians were the last to besiege Tyre, Ezekiel's prophecy would hardly be fulfilled, for *none* of its unusual statements were fulfilled then. But neither does our passage apply these to Nebuchadnezzar, but rather to the "many nations." Were these fulfilled? Let us move on to the next major event in Tyre's history.

Alexander the Great drastically reshaped the Middle East in the late fourth century BC, producing a significant mixing of eastern and western cultures. Crossing the Hellespont with a small army in 334 BC, he secured Asia Minor by destroying two large Persian armies. Alexander then marched southward through Syria towards Egypt, forcing the coastal states into submission. In the process, he succeeded in one of the most dramatic sieges in military history -- at Tyre.

The details of Alexander's conquests are well documented.[3] During the expedition a Day Book of his activities was kept by Eumenes and Diodotus, from which a more polished history was written by Callisthenes of Olynthus. Shortly after Alexander died in 323 BC, two independent histories were written using Callisthenes: one by Aristobolus and another by Ptolemy son of Lagur. Unfortunately, we have none of these records today. However, five other accounts from several centuries later do survive, by Arrian, Diodorus Siculus, Curtius, Justin and Plutarch. Arrian, for instance, writing in the second century AD, uses Aristobolus and Ptolemy as prime sources. Consequently, we still have extensive though secondary accounts from which to learn details of the siege.

What did happen at Tyre in 332 BC, more than two centuries after Ezekiel wrote the prophecies of chapter 26? A most fascinating confrontation between the mighty land forces of Alexander and the unbroken maritime power of Tyre.

Alexander was unwilling to leave the strength of Tyre behind him as he went on to Egypt, lest it be used by the Persians or the Tyrians themselves to destroy his communications with Greece. The Tyrians had no desire to tangle with Alexander, but neither did they intend to give up their liberties if they could avoid it. They sent envoys to Alexander to negotiate an agreement, but (according to Arrian) the Tyrians would allow no Greeks inside their island city.[4] At this time the coastal city of Old Tyre still lay in ruins from Nebuchadnezzar's siege 250 years before, and the Tyrians kept their main strength on the island.

Perhaps as a tactic to gain entry to the city, Alexander asked permission to offer sacrifice to Hercules, the patron god of Tyre. Tyre politely refused, according to Curtius:[5]

> The envoys [from Tyre] replied that there was a temple of
> Hercules outside the city, in the place which they called Old
> Tyre; that there the king would properly offer sacrifice to the
> god. Alexander could not restrain his anger, which as a rule he

was unable to control.

So Alexander decided to take Insular Tyre -- a most formidable task which neither the Assyrians nor Babylonians had managed. To make things worse, Alexander had no navy. How could he engage his army against an island half a mile off the coast? Diodorus reports the situation vividly:[6]

> The king [Alexander] saw that the city could hardly be taken by sea because of the engines mounted along its walls and the fleet that it possessed, while from the land it was almost unassailable... Immediately, he demolished what was called Old Tyre and set many tens of thousands of men to work carrying stones to construct a mole [causeway] two plethra [200 ft] in width. He drafted into service the entire population of the neighboring cities and the project advanced rapidly because the workers were numerous.

So Alexander used the ruins of *Old Tyre* to build a causeway connecting the coast to the island, and he employed many other nations to do it! Curtius states that "a great amount of rocks was available, supplied by Old Tyre..."[7] The ruins of Old Tyre were literally dumped into the sea. Ezekiel could hardly have said it more precisely (vv 4 and 12).

What about the predictions of slaughter and plunder? After Alexander's Macedonians broke through the wall of the island city, Diodorus reports that Alexander[8]

> ...brought down a considerable portion of the wall; and when Macedonians entered through this breach and Alexander's party poured over the bridge onto the wall, the city was taken. The Tyrians, however, kept up the resistance with mutual cries of encouragement, and blocked the alleys with barricades, so that all except a few were cut down fighting, in number more than seven thousand.

Alexander sold the women and children into slavery [9] and crucified all the men of military age, not less than two thousand. The Macedonians were so outraged by Tyre, which had continually provoked them during the siege, that a sickening slaughter resulted. The siege had lasted seven months. As suggested above, *many nations* participated with Alexander in his assault. In addition to his own multinational forces, he drafted the resources of several other states, including former allies of Tyre. Sidon and Cyprus, for instance, supplied ships.[10] After Alexander had decimated Tyre, few other nations resisted his advance. As Ezekiel said, "then all the princes of the coast will step down from their thrones..." (v 16; note also v 18).

If we compare the non-biblical accounts of the siege of Tyre with the prophecy, we can hardly imagine even the most perceptive analyst writing the prophecy more than two centuries before Alexander and describing such an unusual situation so accurately without divine aid. The only purely naturalistic explanation available is that the prophecy must have been written after the event and faked as a prediction. In this case, the date given in the text would have to be false. But this suggestion goes against an impressive amount of evidence which we will discuss in the next section. Thus we are brought to the realization that *the only alternative* (in agreement with the claims of the Bible itself [Deuteronomy 18, Isaiah 41]), is that there really is a God who has chosen to reveal himself through his prophets by means of such predictions.

The history of Tyre does not end with Alexander, however. Consider only one additional event. After conquering Tyre, Alexander had repopulated it with Carians and put it under the control of his Macedonians. After Alexander died in 323, these new residents rebelled against Antigonus, one of Alexander's generals who was attempting to take over his empire. According to Diodorus, Antigonus camped at Old Tyre to besiege Insular Tyre. With the help of 100 ships provided by Seleucus, he established shipyards at Tripolus, Byblus and Sidon.[11] After fourteen months, Insular Tyre surrendered. In the light of our prophecy, this incident is valuable for the information it provides about Old Tyre on shore. At that time it was no more than a campground. Old Tyre remained desolate during this period and has never since been rebuilt. On the former island, now a peninsula since Alexander built his causeway, only a small town remains. This fact is in remarkable harmony with Ezekiel's prophecy.

The Date and Integrity of Ezekiel 26

A crucial point in our argument above is the claim that the prophecy of Ezekiel 26 against Tyre was written before, not after, its fulfillment. It is far easier (and no evidence of divine inspiration) to make "predictions" after an event than before! Thus we must consider the authenticity and integrity of the passage. Was Ezekiel 26 written, as it claims to have been, in the early sixth century BC by the prophet Ezekiel? Since few will claim that the passage was written before the event but not by Ezekiel, let us consider both authorship and date together.

Ezekiel was a contemporary of Nebuchadnezzar. He continued to live after the siege of Tyre ended, since Ezek 29:17 is dated in the 27th year which, according to the chronology of Josephus, would be after the siege. Thus we cannot tell whether Ezekiel wrote this particular prophecy before or after Nebuchadnezzar's siege except from Ezekiel's own dates. We can only observe that there are no contradictions with our interpretation. But the relation of Ezekiel to Alexander is quite different, since the two are separated by nearly 250 years. The predictions about Alexander, if written by Ezekiel, are thus miraculous prophecies or unbelievable guesses!

Before the eighteenth century, few questioned biblical claims regarding authorship. Since then, however, critics have often insisted that some biblical books were written much later than the books themselves claimed, and that some books were written over a period of centuries by several authors. Yet even among the more ardent critics, Ezekiel has maintained a remarkable position. Robert Pfeiffer, reviewing the critical attitude toward Ezekiel in 1941, stated:

> Until recent years few critics questioned the unity of the book and the data on authorship and date which it abundantly supplies. W. W. Baudissin (*Einleitung vor die Bucher des Alten Testament*, p 461) unquestionably gave expression to views generally held when he said, "It can hardly be doubted that the Book of Ezekiel was written by one and the same hand..." The date of its composition is also certain.[12]

This position was not adopted uncritically. The book is most carefully dated and organized, each section giving the year, month and sometimes even the day on which Ezekiel claimed he received his vision from God. Yet the arrangement is not simply chronological. Several subsections are not in chronological order, but grouped by topic instead. Such an arrangement would not likely be adopted by an editor compiling the book centuries later.

Conservative scholar Robert Dick Wilson noted of Ezekiel: "His book is the one document of the Old Testament that the critics accept in its entirety, their theories being built largely upon it."[13] Ezekiel's historical structure has been used as a model to point up alleged weaknesses in other biblical literature. The book has provided a framework for theories dating the various proposed authors of the Pentateuch. Thus the critics cannot well discredit the book without sawing off the limb on which they are sitting!

Even so, Ezekiel has recently come under critical attack, though usually this involves only the latter chapters of the book, not 26. Oeder, for example, thought Ezekiel 40-48 was spurious.[14] Not until Holscher was radical treatment proposed; he claimed that less than 170 of the book's 1,273 verses went back to the "poet" Ezekiel.[15] Even the liberal authors of *The Interpreter's Bible* think this is going too far! However, Holscher himself assigns the rest of the book to an editor living between 500 and 450 BC,[16] which is still more than a century before Alexander and does not avoid the problem of real prediction in Ezekiel 26.

In any case, critical scholars generally reject Holscher's analysis as without foundation:

> One of the most impressive aspects of the book [Ezekiel], despite the opinion of some scholars, is its considerable homogeneity. This is seen in the repetitious phraseology and is also evidenced in ideological content at many points.[17]

Referring to literary parallels, they continue:
> These and other expressions illustrate the complex and numerous interrelationships among the various parts of the book of Ezekiel, and make it impossible objectively to presume a multiplicity of authors.[18]

Thus critics generally reject any major editorial work on the book.

Because of this impressive unity of the book, some critical scholars have concluded that it was written by a single person, but at a time later than Ezekiel's. The most extreme of such views is that of C. C. Torrey, who dates the whole book to 230 BC.[19] This, of course, is well after 332 BC, the latest date for real prediction. But Torrey's view (and others like it) have been criticized by the great majority even of liberal Old Testament scholars as self-contradictory and without justification. For instance, Spiegel remarks:
> Torrey condemns, with Hitzig, the entire cycle of dates in the book as "unecht und willkurlich erronnen" [false and intentionally misleading]. The pang it cost to abandon the whole series as unauthentic he tries to alleviate by a conjecture that permits some element to be genuine: while the years "are of course one and all false,... the *months and days*, on the contrary, may very possibly be those of the original work." The support the author believes himself to have found for this hypothesis is entirely unconvincing.[20]

For instance, Torrey says that our passage clearly and in detail refers to the siege by Alexander, since it was written after the event. Yet Torrey continues on to say that this pseudo-Ezekiel completely blundered in attributing a successful siege to Nebuchadnezzar and not to Alexander. As we pointed out above and as Spiegel notes, the passage itself does not attribute the plundering of Tyre to Nebuchadnezzar. Spiegel also points out that if Torrey is correct and the passage was written after Alexander, there is no reason why pseudo-Ezekiel should make the error Torrey claims he does. Torrey must imagine a writer who is simultaneously misinformed and feebleminded, yet really knowledgeable about ancient history.[21] A theory which needs such contradictions and still so poorly explains the historical content of Ezekiel can hardly stand. Pfeiffer agrees: "The extreme scepticism of critics who, like C. C. Torrey, regard Ezekiel the son of Buzi as a purely imaginary character... is hardly justified."[22]

In particular, chapter 26, the prophecy against Tyre, is regarded by critics as truly authentic and written in the sixth century as claimed. For instance, Cooke claims there can be no doubt about the authenticity of the poetical sections (chs 26-29).[23] Eichrodt, speaking of 26:1-6, says "the careful method of construction of the whole section in forms found elsewhere in Ezekiel is a clear indication of the composition by the prophet's own hand."[24] A full summary of the history of criticism of

Ezekiel is given by Harrison,[25] who feels the integrity of the book is beyond doubt.

Thus centuries of scholarship have found no good reason to date the book later than the time of Ezekiel. Instead it has been regarded as a remarkably historical book. And chapter 26 is in a privileged category in this privileged book. We can say with confidence that the prophecy of chapter 26 was written long before Alexander began his career.

Conclusions

If Ezekiel was written in the sixth century, why is the fulfillment of these predictions in chapter 26 are not mentioned by critical scholars? Alternatively, how do they avoid this remarkable fulfillment? We offer only the briefest analysis.

Our suggestion that the second section of the prophecy refers to Alexander is not unknown in critical circles.[26] Many simply do not comment on the fulfillment. Others feel that the entire passage *must* be explained in terms of Nebuchadnezzar's siege, so they treat the predictions as mistaken prophecy, since Ezekiel 26 was not fulfilled then. To justify such a view, they claim that the switch from singular to plural pronouns between sections two and three is merely a poetic device. As indicated above, this suggestion does not fit the structure of the passage.

Another alternative is proposed by Oxtoby. He claims that the prophecy demands Nebuchadnezzar take *Insular* Tyre, and so dismisses the prophecy as mistaken: "But Nebuchadnezzar did not take Tyre. His siege failed."[27] Oxtoby never once admits the possibility that Ezekiel could be referring to Alexander. He has chosen artificially to force a contradiction on the passage. A good debating technique, but hardly a sound research method!

Let us summarize. First of all, the prophecy against Tyre is indeed unusual and detailed, containing many elements which surpass the best that human ability could foretell.

Second, evidence for the date of writing points to a time centuries before the fulfillment of the major part of the prophecy. There is no evidence for the editing of Ezekiel close to or after the time of Alexander, while much exists for a sixth century BC date. Of course, one can always argue that this conclusion can never be absolutely certain, and therefore allow the assumption that prophecy *cannot* occur to overrule all other evidence. Such an approach will probably be immune to any contrary evidence prior to the second coming of Christ or (equally disastrous) the appearance of a miracle-working Antichrist.

Third, historical records narrating events fulfilling these prophecies are detailed and well-documented, particularly with respect to the most unusual statements. These narratives are in full agreement with the prophecies, and they were not written by Christians, Jews or Muslims who might be suspected of trying to make Ezekiel look good.

What conclusions should we draw? The Bible claims Ezekiel is God's spokesman, that God himself has communicated with us through this prophet. In the fulfillment of prophecies such as these, God reveals his own existence and authenticates his prophets along with their messages. The Bible believer, then, is not blindly trusting anyone who *claims* to have had a revelation. He or she is accepting Scripture on the basis of strong verification that it comes from One who knows, the God who controls history.

Chapter 4

Alexander's Conquest
of Palestine

Perry G. Phillips

Can it be that the prophet Zechariah, in the ninth chapter of his book, predicted details of Alexander's invasion nearly 200 years before it happened? Yes! In this chapter we shall establish the date his predictions were made and see how they were fulfilled in history. First we shall look at the prophet Zechariah and his book. Then we will examine critical problems raised against the unity and authorship of Zechariah 9-14. Finally, we shall discuss Zech 9:1-8 verse by verse, showing how it was fulfilled in Alexander's invasion.

Zechariah and his Book

The prophet Zechariah was apparently a grandson of that Iddo who was chief of a priestly family which returned from Babylonian exile about 536 BC. Zechariah himself began his prophetic ministry as a young man (Zech 1:1; 2:4), in the second year of Darius I (about 520 BC). We do not know how long his prophetic ministry lasted, though his latest dated prophecy is only about two years after this.

The main themes of Zechariah's prophecies are (1) the overthrow of Israel's enemies, (2) the exaltation of Zion (Jerusalem), and (3) the universal reign of the future Messiah. The book easily divides into five sections: (1) a call to repentance (1:1-6); (2) eight symbolic visions with their revealed interpretations (1:7-6:8); (3) questions concerning fasting and God's answer (chs 7-8); (4) the destruction of pagan powers (chs 9-11); and (5) the future of Israel (chs 12-14).

Criticism of Zechariah 9-14

Nearly all scholars accept chapters 1-8 as really by Zechariah. Liberal scholars, however, frequently assign chapters 9-14 to various authors and time-periods.

Some date Zechariah 9-14 to an time earlier than chapters 1-8, *before* the Babylonian captivity. In 1653, Joseph Mede noticed that the prophecy mentioned in Matt 27:9-10 was a free rendition of Zech 11:12-13, yet the Gospel writer mentions Jeremiah instead. Mede concluded that Zechariah 9-11 was pre-exilic,[1] and he was followed by Bishop Kidder (1700) and William Whiston (1722). Archbishop Newcome put chapters 9-11 even earlier, in the eighth century BC, just before the fall of the

Northern Kingdom to Assyria. Newcome's view spread to Germany, where Berthold argued for an eighth century date for the whole of chapters 9-14. He suggested its author was *another* Zechariah, son of Jeberekiah, mentioned in Isa 8:2. The idea that Zechariah 9-14 was written before the exile appealed to a number of notable nineteenth century critics such as Hitzig, Knobel, Ewald, Bleek, Von Orelli and Schultz.[2]

More common today is the claim that Zechariah 9-14 was written *much later* than the time of Zechariah, in Hellenistic or Maccabean times (330-150 BC). The pre-exilic dating was challenged by Corrodi in 1792 and by Paulus in 1805. Eichhorn (1824) suggested that Zech 9:1-10:12 described the invasion of Alexander the Great (332 BC), and that Zech 13:7-14:21 referred to the death of Judah the Maccabee (161 BC). DeWette, who previously held a pre-exilic date, also switched to a late date. Other nineteenth century critics who placed these chapters in Hellenistic times were Cornill, Wellhausen, Eckhardt, Cheyne, Kirkpatrick and Driver. The pre-exilic date, once hailed as a sure result of higher criticism, was rejected after a reign of only fifty years.

The main argument raised against a single author for the whole book of Zechariah concerns the marked contrast between Zechariah 1-8 and 9-14. As our concern here is fulfillment of prophecy, we will not respond to views which date chs 9-14 before the time of Alexander. Below we give a summary of the main late-date arguments together with brief refutations.

1. The reference to *Greece* in 9:13 is often thought to reflect the time of Seleucid Greek control over Jerusalem. Since this did not occur until after Alexander, the passage 9:1-10:2 is dated between 300-165 BC.

Greek influence, however, was felt in the Near East as early as the seventh century BC. Greek mercenary troops had been employed by the Persians, though they perpetually feuded with their commanders. Greek raids on the Palestinian coast also occurred at this time. In 500 BC, the Greeks of Ionia revolted against the Persians. The next year, the Athenians burned the Persian stronghold at Sardis. Then the Greeks successfully turned back Persian invasions at Marathon in 490 and Salamis in 480. Since Zechariah was a "young man" (2:4) when his ministry began in 520, he may well have lived to see the rise of Greek power in the West. Liberals usually claim the author of Isa 55-66 was a contemporary of the actual Zechariah, yet Isa 66:19 also mentions Greece.[3] A reference to Greece is thus no evidence for dating Zech 9-14 in the Hellenistic period.

2. Good and evil *shepherds* are mentioned in Zech 11:4-17 and 13:7-9. Various historical identifications have been proposed. Some see the Jewish high priest Onias IV as the good shepherd, Alcimus as the evil shepherd, and Lysimachus, Jason and Menelaus as the three evil shepherds. Others see Onias III as the good shepherd, Menelaus as the

evil shepherd, and the rejection of the three evil shepherds as Onias III driving out Simon, Menelaus and Lysimachus. The former view dates the passage about 160 BC; the latter about 150-140 BC.

No fewer than *thirty* different identifications have been proposed for the three evil shepherds! Clearly, considerable guesswork is involved in identifying the figures in Zechariah 11 with specific individuals of the Maccabean period, not least of which is the assumption that the figures refer to people living at the author's own time.[4]

3. Zechariah 12-14 contains so-called *apocalyptic* material, i.e., prophecy characterized by bold symbolism, world-shaking events, sharp good/evil conflict, end-time judgment and resurrection. Liberal scholars generally assign apocalyptic literature to the intertestament period, after about 200 BC.

But Ladd[5] and Bright[6] have shown that apocalyptic material is found throughout the Old Testament, some of it from long before the Maccabean period. Hence, to date writings on the basis of apocalyptic content is invalid.

Against these arguments for another, later author of Zechariah 9-14, consider the following evidence for a single author of the entire book.

1. Both sections (chs 1-8 and 9-14) contain the same general *subject matter*: (1) the necessity for repentance and cleansing (1:4; 3:4,9; 5:1ff; and 13:1,9); (2) the return of Israel (2:6-7; 8:7; and 10:6-12); (3) the overthrow and conversion of Israel's enemies (1:21; 2:8-9; 8:20-23; and 9:1-8; 12:4; 14:16); and (4) the hope of a Messianic deliverer/ruler (6:12-13 and 9:9-10).

2. Both sections have a similar *style*, for instance (1) the symbolic use of "two" (4:3; 5:9; 6:1; and 11:7; 13:8); and (2) the vocative form of address (2:7,10; 3:2,8; 4:7; and 9:9,13; 11:1ff; 13:7). The phrase "pass through and return" occurs in 7:14 and 9:8, but nowhere else in Scripture.

3. There is a tendency to *dwell* on an idea, as in 6:10,11,13 (take ... take; throne ... throne); 8:4-5 (streets ... streets); and 14:5 (you will flee ... yea, you will flee).

4. Zechariah has an *evangelistic* emphasis in both sections.

5. The language of both sections is remarkably free from *Aramaisms*. Given that the Jews spoke Aramaic as their native language in the intertestament period, this would not be expected if Zechariah were written then.

6. *Chiasm* is a poetic device by which lines or elements are paired in reversed order. For example, with six lines of poetry, instead of the parallel lines *a/a', b/b'* and *c/c'* being ordered *aa'bb'cc'* or *abca'b'c'*, in chiasm the order would be *abcc'b'a'*. A five-element chiastic structure appears in both sections of Zechariah (6:13; and 9:5; 9:7; 12:4). This suggests a deep underlying unity of the two parts of the book.[7]

7. A fragmentary Greek manuscript of Zechariah has been found among the *Dead Sea Scrolls*. The fact that it contains the transition from

8:23 to 9:1 argues for the unity of parts. The early date of the manuscript also provides evidence against a Maccabean date for the book.[8]

8. Finally, those who reject the Zecharian authorship of chs 9-14 have not been able to agree upon an *alternate theory* of composition. By implication, no suitable alternative to single authorship for the whole book has been found.

We conclude that the internal evidence strongly favors unity of authorship. Since there is no external evidence to the contrary, we may confidently ascribe the book to "Zechariah, son of Berechiah, son of Iddo," writing about the end of the sixth century BC.

Analysis and Fulfillment of Zech 9:1-8

Before we go through the passage verse by verse, we give our own literal translation:

(1) The burden of the word of the LORD in the land of Hadrach and Damascus its resting place. (For to the LORD are the eyes of man and all the tribes of Israel.)

(2) And also Hamath, which borders thereby. Tyre and Sidon, for she is very wise.

(3) For Tyre has built herself a stronghold and she has heaped up silver like dust and gold like mire in the streets.

(4) Behold! The Lord will dispossess her and he will smite her strength in the sea and she will be consumed with fire.

(5) Ashkelon will see [this] and be afraid, and Gaza will writhe in great pain; and Ekron [too], for her confidence was dried up. And a king will perish from Gaza and Ashkelon will not be inhabited.

(6) And a strange race will live in Ashdod and I will cut off the pride of the Philistines.

(7) And I will remove his blood from before him [lit., "from his face"], and his detestable things from his teeth, and even he will be a remnant to our God, and he will be as a chief in Judah, and Ekron [will be] as a Jebusite.

(8) And I will encamp as a guard for my house from him who is passing through and returning, and an oppressor will not pass through them again. For now I have seen it with my eyes.

Briefly, the prophecy begins in Syria, and then broadens out to include Phoenicia and Philistia, naming the various cities. The magnificent city of Tyre will be overthrown. The destruction of the Philistine cities will result in the loss of their pride. The Lord will take away the objectionable features of Philistine worship, while incorporating a remnant of the Philistines into Israel. Eventually, Israel will be safe from all external harassment, for the Lord himself will be her guard.

Verses 1-8 form a literary unit. The first four verses deal with northern cities; the last four with southern cities. Each end (vv 1-2a and 7b-8) proclaims salvation, whereas the middle (2b-7a) pronounces judgment. The "eyes" motif of v 1 is balanced by that in v 8. The passage itself fits into a well-balanced structure underlying all of Zechariah 9-14.⁹ Baldwin summarizes Lamarche's analysis as follows:

> The introductory subject, judgment and salvation of neighboring peoples (9:1-8) a, is balanced by the conclusion, in which the theme includes all nations (14:16-21) a'. In the remaining material, which divides into two sections at the end of chapter 11, three themes may be distinguished: b, the king, the shepherd and the Lord's representative, all of whom are identified as one and the same person; c, Israel's war and victory; d, judgment on idols. These themes form the following pattern in the text: b (9:9-10), c (9:11-10:1), d (10:2-3a), c' (10:3b-11:3), b' (11:4-17). In the second half the order is inverted: c" (12:1-9), b" (12:10-13:1), d' (13:2-6), b''' (13:7-9), c'''(14:1-15).¹⁰

It is difficult to see how such a well-ordered arrangement could have arisen if Zechariah 9-14 were merely an anthology of two or more authors writing at various times. The unity of this section and its parallels to Zechariah 1-8 form a most convincing argument for single authorship for the entire book!

Let us move on to a verse-by-verse analysis of the prophecy.

Verse 1. The burden of the word of the LORD in the land of Hₐdrach and Damascus its resting place. (For to the LORD are the eyes of man and all the tribes of Israel.)

There is some question whether the Hebrew *b'eretz* means "in the land" or "against the land."¹¹ If the former is intended, the prophet may be giving the location of his vision. Though Zechariah began his ministry in Judah and Jerusalem (Ezra 5:1), he might have taken a trip to Syria to visit and encourage the Israelites from the northern tribes who had been taken captive "beyond Damascus" (Amos 5:27). Their expectation of restoration to Israel would explain the expression concerning all eyes being on the LORD.

Most commentators feel "against the land" is intended. Then the judgment upon Syria was fulfilled when Damascus surrendered to Parmenio, one of Alexander's generals, after Alexander's victory at the battle of Issus.¹²

The land of Hadrach is in northern Syria and is only mentioned this one time in the Bible. Perhaps it is the city of Hatarileka mentioned as fighting the Assyrians in the eighth century BC.¹³

The expression we have translated "to the LORD are the eyes of man and all the tribes of Israel" is translated by some as "the eyes of the LORD are upon man and all the tribes of Israel."¹⁴ But the former, more literal rendering is quite acceptable. "Both the people generally and the

Israelites in this region look to the prophet as to one through whom Yahweh has chosen to speak."[15]

Verse 2. And also Hamath, which borders thereby. Tyre and Sidon, for she is very wise.

Hamath is on the Orontes River between Hadrach and Damascus.

Though the prophet names Tyre and Sidon together, one wonders why "she is very wise" is singular. Grammatically, it is most natural to associate the phrase with Sidon. This also fits the context, where it is clear from vv 3-4 that Tyre is destroyed, while nothing of the sort is said of Sidon. Could it be that Sidon's wisdom was displayed in some way which kept her from being overthrown? Was Sidon wise enough to save herself by *not* relying on her fortifications as Tyre did? May not the prophet be contrasting Tyre -- the mighty city that fell -- with Sidon -- the wise city which remained? If so, what was Sidon's act of wisdom?

After Alexander conquered Syria, he turned toward the Phoenician cities of Tyre and Sidon. The Sidonians surrendered to him, but the Tyrians decided to fight instead. The disastrous result of this decision for Tyre has been described in the previous chapter,[16] which shows Sidon's wisdom in not resisting!

Verse 3. For Tyre has built herself a stronghold and she has heaped up silver like dust and gold like mire in the streets.

Here we have a play on words in the Hebrew, between Tyre, *tsor* and stronghold, *matsowr*. Tyre's military might caused Alexander considerable trouble. Her wealth was proverbial (Ezek 28:2-8).

Verse 4. Behold! The Lord will dispossess her and he will smite her strength in the sea and she will be consumed with fire.

Alexander was aided by supernatural strength and wisdom. As Baron suggests:

> Though Tyre is so wise, so doubly strong, so rich -- yea, even though her strength were a hundred times as great, and she enclosed herself in a hundred strong walls of one hundred and fifty feet high, "*the Lord* will dispossess her"; for cities or peoples cannot barricade themselves against God, and "it is altogether useless to build strongholds to keep *Him* out." It was *the Lord* who did it through Alexander, whom he used as a scourge against Phoenicia and the Persian power at that time.[17]

Tyre depended heavily on her navy to save herself from Alexander. For as Arrian points out:

> The city was an island and strengthened all round with a high wall; moreover, any movements from the seaward side were in Tyre's favor, as the Persians were still supreme at sea and the Tyrians had plenty of ships left.[18]

The Tyrians gave Alexander considerable trouble, "being still masters of the sea."[19] Nevertheless, even her strong navy was finally "smitten."

Curtius specifically notes that after Alexander's victory he "gave orders that all except those who had taken refuge in the temples should be slain and the houses set on fire."[20] Truly, Tyre was "consumed with fire."

One is hard-pressed to dismiss the detailed fulfillment of the prophecy against Tyre as mere coincidence.

Verse 5. Ashkelon will see [this] and be afraid, and Gaza will writhe in great pain; and Ekron [too], for her confidence was dried up. And a king will perish from Gaza and Ashkelon will not be inhabited.

Although the context would seem to favor the abandonment of Ashkelon at the time of Alexander, it does not demand it. Perhaps "Ashkelon will not be inhabited" refers to some brief abandonment of the city at his approach, though there is no explicit reference to this in the historians. Since the verb is a Hebrew imperfect, it may refer to some event further in the future. In actuality, Ashkelon became a center of Hellenistic culture, and continued with the usual vicissitudes of cities in that part of the world until it was dismantled by Sultan Baibars in 1270 AD. Since then it has remained a ruin, perhaps in this way fulfilling Zechariah's prophecy.

Gaza, on the other hand, was destroyed at Alexander's coming. Olmstead gives the details:

> Gaza proper lay two and a half miles inland and was separated from the shore by deep sand; it was a large city with a strong wall along the edge of the high mound which covered the debris of much earlier predecessors. First Alexander ordered a counterwall against the south side of the city; after he had been wounded, he completed the circumvallation by a wall a quarter of a mile broad and two hundred and fifty feet high. Engines and tunnels employed by the defense proved of no avail; at last the walls were scaled and the gates opened from within. The garrison still fought on, and all died at their posts. With the usual barbarity, the women and children taken were sold as slaves. The site was handed over to the neighbor tribes, but Gaza itself remained uninhabited. Hundreds of talents of myrrh and frankincense were carried off as loot, a heavy loss to Nabataean merchants.[21]

Of particular interest is the end of King Betis of Gaza. He was tied by his heels to Alexander's chariot and dragged through the city. Truly "a king will perish from Gaza."

Ekron was the northernmost of the four Philistine cities, and would be the first to suffer if Tyre fell. She must have lost all confidence at the news of Tyre's destruction, as would Gaza and Ashkelon.

Verse 6. And a strange race will live in Ashdod and I will cut off the pride of the Philistines.

Literally *mamzer*, translated "strange race," means an illegitimate child (Deut 23:2). The Greek Septuagint translation uses *allogeneis*,

"other races," such as were already living there in Nehemiah's time (Neh
13:24).   During the Maccabean period, Ashdod (called Azodus) was
devastated in turn by Judas (1 Macc 4:15; 5:68), Jonathan (10:84-85) and
John Hyrcanus (16:10). This would certainly account for the Philistines'
loss of pride.   Under Gabinius, the Roman governor about 55 BC,
Ashdod was rebuilt and repopulated as a Roman city.[22] Perhaps the
Romans were the "strange race."

   *Verse 7. And I will remove his blood from before him [lit., "from his
face"], and his detestible things from his teeth, and even he will be a
remnant to our God, and he will be as a chief in Judah, and Ekron [will
be] as a Jebusite.*

   This verse looks beyond the time of Alexander the Great to the
disappearance of the idolatrous practices of the Philistines. The references to blood and "detestable things" picture the heathen practice of eating
meat offered to idols, along with its blood (see Ezek 33:25).   The
references to "remnant" and "chief" indicate that the Philistines would
eventually become a part of Judah. Exactly how or when this happened
is not clear. But this much is known:

   (1) That many proselytes to Judaism were made from among
   these peoples, especially those of Philistia (Josephus, *Antiquities*
   13.15.4); (2) That after the return from Babylonia many of the
   Jews settled in Philistia, intermarriages took place between the
   Jews and the Philistines, and the two peoples gradually assimilated in manners and religion; (3) That in the time of our Lord
   the Philistines were no longer known as a separate nation, but
   what remained of them was mixed up with the Jews, or formed
   part of the undistinguishable population of the country; and (4)
   That the name Philistia, originally the designation only of the
   country of the Philistines, came to be accepted, under the form
   of Palestina, as the name of the whole land, which could not have
   been done had the district of Philistia remained the territory of
   a separate and heathen race hostile to the Jews. In this part of
   the prophecy, therefore, we have a prediction of what actually
   came to pass in later times as exact as ... is consistent with the
   permanent distinction between prophecy and history.[23]

   A further outworking of the Philistine conversion is seen in Acts 8:40,
when the evangelist Philip preached in the cities from Gaza to Caesarea.
The city of Ekron would be incorporated into Judah just as the Jebusites
were incorporated at the time of David (2 Samuel 5). This occurred
when the Seleucid king Alexander Balas gave Ekron to Jonathan in the
Maccabean period. It is significant that Ekron, the most inland of the
above-mentioned cities, did not experience the devastation that fell upon
Ashkelon, Ashdod and Gaza. Yet another example of the precision of
Zechariah's prophecy is seen here.

   Verse 8. And I will encamp as a guard for my house from him who is passing through and returning, and an oppressor will not pass through them again. For now I have seen it with my eyes.

"My house" may refer to the temple, newly rebuilt at the time of Zechariah, or possibly to the entire nation as in Jer 12:7 and Hos 8:1; 9:15. In either case the Lord will protect it from "him who is passing through and returning." Many authors identify this phrase with Alexander's visit to Jerusalem.[24]

According to Josephus,[25] while Alexander was besieging Tyre, he sent a letter to Jaddua, the high priest in Jerusalem, to send provisions to the Macedonians. Jaddua replied that he had given an oath not to bear arms against Darius, the Persian king from whom Alexander was conquering the Middle East. Alexander, angry with Jaddua, threatened to make an expedition to Jerusalem to teach the high priest to whom he should keep his oath. Having taken Gaza, Alexander turned toward Jerusalem.

Jaddua, in fear, asked the people of the city to sacrifice to God and to pray for deliverance. God then spoke to him in a dream and told him to be courageous and go out to meet Alexander. When Jaddua learned that Alexander was close to the city, he led a procession of priests and white-robed citizens out to meet him. Upon seeing the high priest arrayed in his purple and scarlet robes, with the mitre on his head having the gold plate with God's name on it, Alexander greeted Jaddua and adored God's name. When asked why he honored the Jewish high priest, Alexander replied that God had revealed to him in a dream in Macedonia that one dressed as the high priest was would be the servant of God.

Alexander was subsequently led into Jerusalem and offered sacrifice at the temple. He was glad when they showed him the book of Daniel predicting the victory of the Greeks over the Persians (ch 8). He gave the Jews the right to observe their own laws and to enlist in his army. Alexander then left Jerusalem to resume his battle against Darius.

The historicity of this account has been questioned. For example, Josephus states that Alexander visited Jerusalem on his way to Egypt, whereas Arrian[26] and Curtius[27] say Alexander went directly to Egypt in a week. Also Albright thinks it unlikely that Jaddua would have been high priest in 332 BC, since his father was already high priest eighty years earlier.[28]

Nevertheless, as Pusey remarks:

> The facts remain; that the conqueror, who, above most, gave way to his anger, bestowed privileges almost incredible on a nation, which under the Medes and Persians had been "the most despised part of the enslaved" (Tacitus, *Histories* 5.8); made them equal in privileges to his own Macedonians, who could hardly brook the absorption of the Persians, although in inferior condition, among themselves. The most despised of the enslaved became the most trusted of the trusted. They became a large portion of the second and third then known cities of the world.

They became Alexandrians, Antiochenes, Ephesians without ceasing to be Jews. The law commanded faithfulness to oaths, and they who despised their religion respected its fruits.[29]

Though the above account, if genuine, fits well with Zechariah's prophecy, its complete fulfillment is best seen in that glorious future when Jerusalem will be forever free from oppression.

Conclusions

We have shown that the material in Zechariah 9-14 was written near the end of the sixth century BC. Therefore Zech 9:1-8 is a real prediction concerning Alexander's sweep through Phoenicia and Philistia. The intricate details relating to this prophecy were fulfilled: Tyre was destroyed, whereas Sidon was spared. Ashkelon, Ashdod and Gaza experienced destruction; Ekron was assimilated into Judah. Nations were conquered and peoples were displaced, but the Jews were greatly honored and respected.

The fulfillment of Zechariah's prophecy adds to the evidence God has provided that he really exists and that he has revealed himself in the Bible. It is he who sent his son Jesus Christ to die on the cross that all who trust in him might be reconciled to God. May you, reading these words, be encouraged to turn to him as Savior and honor him as Lord.

Chapter 5

The Fall of Nineveh

Elaine A. Phillips

The downfall of Nineveh, capital of the mighty but cruel Assyrian empire, is predicted with great vividness by the prophet Nahum in one of the shorter books of the Old Testament. The striking fulfillment of Nahum's many specific prophecies, which we shall examine later in this chapter, puts pressure upon those who refuse to believe in such a thing as fulfilled prophecy.

Rejection of supernatural prediction, unfortunately, dominates scholarship today, both secular and religious. Because of this bias, critics deny the authenticity of Nahum and other Old Testament prophetic books to avoid such predictions. Among various methods used to discredit prophecy, a common one is to claim that the prophecy was actually given *after* the event which it allegedly predicts.[1] In fairness to those who seriously wish to know whether or not there is real prediction in the Bible, we must spend some time establishing, as accurately as possible, a date for Nahum's prophecy.

Before we discuss the date of Nahum directly, however, there are two related matters which we must consider first: the unity of the book and its historical background.

The Unity of the Book of Nahum

It is easy to see why we must investigate the unity of Nahum. If one does not believe the book was written as a single whole, then whenever something begins to look too much like a fulfilled prediction, the critic may say that the particular passage is merely a later addition, the activity of a redactor or editor.

For the book of Nahum in particular, this problem frequently crops up. Many scholars claim that the first chapter is an acrostic psalm, each verse beginning with a letter of the Hebrew alphabet, in alphabetical order, which was added to the book later. Pfeiffer's view is typical:

A redactor living about the year 300 BC prefaced Nahum's superb ode, dating from the years immediately preceding the fall of Nineveh in 612 BC, with an alphabetic psalm of his own time.[2]

Coming from a widely recognized scholar, this statement sounds impressive until we notice two serious problems. First, critics do not agree on the extent of the acrostic. Some say it is incomplete, running only through 1:10. Others claim it continues into chapter 2, but it is in a sad state of disrepair. Second, even the first half of this alleged acrostic is very incomplete and mixed up. To illustrate, the first nine letters of the

Hebrew alphabet are: *aleph, beth, gimel, daleth, he, waw, zayin, heth, teth*. In the acrostic, therefore, one would expect the first nine verses (vv 2-10, since v 1 is the superscription) to begin with these letters. Instead, the actual sequence is: *aleph, yodh, gimel, he, lamedh, teth, waw, mem, caph*. Of the nine letters, only four belong to the first nine letters of the alphabet, and only two are in the right locations! To solve this problem, Pfeiffer says:

> Of this psalm he [the redactor] vaguely remembered the first part, substituting for the rest remarks of his own, some of which were Biblical quotations quoted from memory.... It is clear that he did not copy the alphabetic psalm from a manuscript but wrote it down as best he could from memory. He had not only forgotten the second part of the poem, but he paraphrased certain lines, thereby obliterating the original acrostic structure.[3]

When we must assume the existence of a redactor with a memory so faulty as to forget the (obvious) alphabetic structure of a poem he thought important enough to add to the work of a respected prophet, and with insufficient ability or ambition to find a manuscript of the poem or compose his own verses starting with the right letters of the alphabet, it is time to be suspicious of our presuppositions! Given the evidence of the text, it is highly unlikely there was ever any acrostic poem involved in the first place.[4]

The claim that the book of Nahum has been added to by means of *interpolation* is more difficult to refute. Obviously, if a critic thinks it acceptable to begin dissecting the text, there is no stopping him. Whenever something does not agree with his presuppositions, he *discovers* an insertion. Nevertheless, let us suggest some of the problems with this approach through specific examples.

Nahum 1:13 says, "So now, I will break off his yoke bar from upon you, and I will tear off your shackles." A reasonable inference from this is that Israel was being oppressed by some particular enemy at the time the statement was written. Given the subject of the book, the enemy would naturally be Nineveh. According to the critic, however, this *cannot* be a part of the original text since, in his view, the original was written about 612 BC when Israel was not under the yoke of any oppressor. Yet critics will not allow that it was written earlier, as this would make the whole book a fulfilled prophecy of the fall of Nineveh. To account for this verse, the critics assign it to a later writer during or after the Babylonian exile, when the nation was being oppressed (though not by Assyria). Needless to say, this is simply a case of letting one's presuppositions determine what the text may say, rather than molding one's views to fit the text. A dangerous game!

To get some perspective on the claims of interpolation, it is helpful to see what is left of a text when alleged interpolations are removed. If the logical continuity is destroyed by such removal, the method itself should be suspect. What happens, for instance, when such critical principles are applied to chapter one? Verses 2 through 10 are removed because they form the acrostic psalm supposedly added later. Verses 12 and 13 are omitted because they refer to some later time when Israel was under oppression. Verse 15 is also omitted as an interpolation. As a result, only three verses (1, 11 and 14) remain as original out of the fifteen! This is already suspicious in itself. When we also consider the thematic connections between chapter one and the rest of the book, not to mention its stylistic and linguistic unity with the rest of the book, it is difficult to accept such wholesale partition. Another example of interpolation alleged by critics is Nahum 3:18-19:

> Your shepherds are sleeping, O king of Assyria / Your nobles are lying down. / Your people are scattered on the mountains, / And there is no one to regather them. / There is no relief for your breakdown, / Your wound is incurable. / All who hear about you / Will clap their hands over you. / For on whom has not your evil passed continually?

Why is this seen as an interpolation? Because after such a vivid description of Nineveh's downfall as has been portrayed in the previous verses, these verses are alleged to be redundant and unnecessary. But as Maier points out:

> Such criticism is prompted only by bias, for the material in these verses is predominantly new.... If vv 18 and 19 be eliminated, the prophecies are deprived of certain remarkable statements. The book would close without saying anything about the final scattering of the Assyrian people in the mountains and about the joy with which the news of the city's end would be greeted.[5]

Evidence -- as opposed to assumptions about the impossibility of prophecy -- points to the conclusion that the book is a single unit. The facts are summarized by Maier:

> ... every verse in the entire three chapters has been assailed by some important critical writer as non-Nahumic. Most modern interpreters remove at least one third of the verses as spurious glosses. In the sections regarded as authentic, every verse has been subjected to drastic alteration, emendation, addition, change of words or phrase order. In this way, some recent exegetical works change at least two thirds of the entire prophecy. These extremes mark the fatal weakness of such radical exegesis, showing both the arbitrary nature of its *modus operandi* [method] and the unsatisfactory force of its conclusions. No other literature on earth has suffered by such arbitrary excisions and additions. Significantly enough... the book of Nahum, when read as preserved [in the Masoretic text], presents a poem, in the Hebrew sense, which for vividness of presentation, order of development, and force of prophetic forecast, stands unexcelled

in all literature.[6]

The Historical Setting of Nahum

Taking the book of Nahum to be a single unit, then, we want to establish the date it was written, using both internal and external evidence. In order better to follow the reasoning for the various proposed dates, we need to look at the historical setting and establish earliest and latest dates beyond which the prophecy could not occur.

Basically, the book is set in the seventh century BC. The political powers it pictures are Assyria, Judah and Egypt. Babylon comes to prominence at the end of this century, but for most of the time it was a vassal state under Assyria.

Let us summarize the history of Assyria in this period. Sargon II of Assyria conquered and destroyed Samaria, the capital city of Israel's Northern Kingdom, in 722 BC; he continued to reign until 705. Sargon was followed by Sennacherib (704-681), who began a great building program at Nineveh. In 680, he was succeeded by Esarhaddon, who reigned to 669. Esarhaddon was followed by Ashurbanipal, who held the empire until 626. Ashurbanipal was the last strong king of Assyria; already in his time the Assyrian empire had begun to weaken. We think the next two Assyrian kings were Ashur-etil-ilani and Sin-shar-ish-kun, both of whom are known by other names as well. Our problem is that the Assyrian chronicles suddenly stop in 648, when things begin to go badly for Assyria. Our knowledge of the fall of Nineveh in 612 -- to Cyaxares the Mede, Nabopolassar the Babylonian, and a horde of Scythians -- comes from the *Babylonian Chronicle*.

During this period, Judah was ruled by Manasseh (692-42), Amon (642-39) and Josiah (639-09). Throughout Manasseh's reign, Judah was subject to Assyria, paying heavy tribute. 2 Chron 33:11 hints that Manasseh tried to rebel, but the attempt failed. Essentially, Manasseh was a tribute-paying vassal of the Assyrians. So was his son, Amon, though some scholars think Amon's murder may have been perpetrated by a growing anti-Assyrian faction in Judah which wanted him out of the way. Whatever the case, by the time Josiah came to power, Assyria was too weak to keep Judah from breaking away. This Assyrian weakness was due to growing internal struggles in the empire.

Meanwhile in Egypt, Ashurbanipal conquered most of the country about 663 BC, sacking the city of Thebes, referred to in Nahum 3:8 as No-Amon. This is recorded in the *Inscriptions of Ashurbanipal*:

(69) I went to Thebes the strong city. (70) The approach of my powerful army he saw, and Thebes he abandoned, (71) and fled to Kiptip. That city [Thebes] (72) the whole of it, in the service of Asshur and Ishtar my hands took; (73) silver, gold,

precious stones, the furniture of his palace, all there was, (74) garments of wool and linen, great horses, (75) people male and female. (76) Two lofty obelisks covered with beautiful carving (77) 2,500 talents [over 90 tons] their weight, standing before the gate of a temple, (78) from their places I removed and brought to Assyria. (79) The spoil great and unnumbered, I carried off from the midst of Thebes.[7]

This historical record serves to verify the account given by Nahum in 3:10:

Even she [Thebes/No-Amon] went into exile in captivity. / Even her babies were dashed to pieces at the head of all the streets. / And for her nobles they cast a lot, / And all her mighty ones were bound in chains.

After the sack of Thebes, Psammetichus I, an Egyptian noble, revolted against the Assyrian oppressors and freed Egypt. He remained a major power until about 610. The Egyptian revolt against Assyria was successful because Ashurbanipal was occupied with troubles caused by Shamash-shum-ukin, his own brother, whom he had made ruler over Babylon. In 650-48, Shamash-shum-ukin allied with Elam in revolt against Ashurbanipal; the latter had to concentrate his forces on this revolt and so could not deal with Egypt and Judah. In regaining control of Babylon, Ashurbanipal committed a greater slaughter than he had in taking Thebes. By the time he was free to deal with Egypt and Judah, both had gained their independence and Assyria was severely weakened. Though Thebes never regained its former prominence, the city was rebuilt and inhabited.[8]

Suggested Dates for Nahum

With this brief historical outline in mind, let us evaluate various dates suggested for the book of Nahum in the light of the political situation. Six different dates will be considered, ranging from about 654 BC (Nahum as author) to the Maccabean period (second century BC). We will consider these here in reverse chronological order.

1. Consider first the suggestion Nahum was written in the *Maccabean period.* The juggling one must do to obtain this date would do credit to a circus performer! In this view, the Nineveh mentioned in Nahum is not the capital of Assyria, but a relatively unimportant city in Northern Mesopotamia. Others see Nineveh as a *code-word* for God's enemy, the Seleucid empire. The reference to Thebes/No-Amon is a *disguised* allusion to the failure of Antiochus Epiphanes to take Alexandria.[9] All this flies in the face of the fact that the book of the twelve minor prophets was known and already highly esteemed by the Maccabean period.[10] Nor is there any evidence that the quality of Hebrew literature written in the

Maccabean period was even close to the high level of Nahum.

2. A second proposal is that Nahum was written *just after* the fall of Nineveh as a song of praise for its destruction. Two problems face this suggestion. (1) The internal evidence of Nahum 2:4-3:17 makes the event still future.[11] (2) In order to be consistent in style, Nahum should have mentioned Nineveh's destroyers by name, just as in 3:9 (referring to a past event) he names Thebes' allies. Most critics avoid the drastic step of claiming the prophecy of Nineveh's destruction was written after the fact. For instance the *International Critical Commentary* (ICC) says:

> That we are not dealing with a *vaticinium post eventum* [prophecy after the fact] is clear: the hope of the prophet is too genuine and fresh; the details of the siege and conquest are too minute and would be somewhat superfluous, to say the least; and the total lack of any shadow cast by the knowledge, or even suspicion, that Babylon was a far more severe taskmaster than Nineveh had ever been would be inexplicable.[12]

3. Instead, the ICC and most critics claim that Nahum was written *just before* the fall of Nineveh in 612. The main reasons given are as follows. (1) Between the time that the Medes, under Cyaxares, first began to trouble the Assyrians by taking Asshur in 614, and the fall of Nineveh in 612, any reasonably intelligent person could see what was coming. Against an early date, Pfeiffer notes, "the openly expressed vindictiveness, implied patriotic fervor, and assurance of Assyria's irretrievable ruin [seen in the book of Nahum] are hardly conceivable before 625."[13] (2) Since the sins of Judah are not mentioned at all, it is more reasonable to suppose Nahum was written after the reforms of Josiah than during the apostasy of Manasseh. (3) Even though the fall of Thebes occurred before 660, it was so dramatic that it would have been remembered and used as an example even fifty years later.

Each of these assertions can be adequately answered. The main problem for this view is that the text of Nahum pictures Israel as under the yoke of an oppressor when the prophecy was given, seen most clearly in 1:12-13. But between 614 and 612 Assyria was oppressing no one. Rather it was trying merely to hold its own against the combined forces of the Medes, Babylonians and Scythians. It was this fact which started the critics partitioning the text in the first place.

Also Nahum describes Assyria as at the height of its power, not as a decadent state. Note, for example, Nahum 3:1, 4, 16:

> Woe to the city of blood, full of lies, full of plunder, never without victims!... alluring, the mistress of sorceries, who enslaved nations by her prostitution, and peoples by her witchcraft.... You have increased the number of your merchants till they are more than the stars of the sky...

This was the situation throughout the reigns of Manasseh and Amon. But shortly after the accession of Josiah, the Assyrian domination was sufficiently weakened that Josiah could quit paying tribute and even invade Samaria to destroy high places there. Yet Josiah came to the throne in 639, long before the time suggested for the writing of Nahum in this view.

The objection (2) regarding the absence of any reference to the sins of Judah is really not very serious. The prophecy, after all, is directed against Nineveh in particular, not against Judah nor sinners in general.

The argument (3) concerning Thebes may also be answered easily. It is true that the sack of Thebes was a terrible event, yet the city itself did not die. On the contrary, it was rebuilt, and Psammetichus I consolidated his forces in the area. Although it never regained its former status, it rose high enough that we hear one of Psammetichus' men designated "prince of Thebes."[14] As a result, the statement of Nahum 3:8 regarding Thebes would have its greatest impact if written shortly after the fall of Thebes about 663 BC. If the prophecy was written about 614-612 as claimed, there would have been more impressive examples of slaughter nearer at hand. Ashurbanipal's ferocity in crushing the revolt at Babylon in 648 would be one such.

4. The fourth proposed date for Nahum is 625. This date was chosen because the critic finds it necessary to locate some historical reason why the prophet should think the city of Nineveh was about to fall. Needless to say, this approach implicitly puts a serious limitation on divine prophecy, as though God could not reveal a disaster to a prophet unless it was already on the horizon and seemed reasonable to the prophet. The historical circumstance which is supposed to have led Nahum to predict the fall of Nineveh is an alleged attack on Nineveh in 625 by Cyaxares, king of the Medes, to which the Greek historian Herodotus makes reference.[15] The historicity of this attack is in doubt at present, so one should not put too much weight on it. In any case, the reasons given above for the inadequacy of 614-612 also apply to this suggestion.

5. The fifth suggestion, 648 BC, has the same motivation as the fourth, but a different occasion. It was in 648 that Babylon revolted against Ashurbanipal under the leadership of Shamash-shum-ukin. Though the revolt did demonstrate the growing difficulties of Assyria, it has serious problems as a date for Nahum:

> ... that revolt [under Shamash-shum-ukin] spread among and included a great many peoples, while the prophecy of Nahum seems to picture the fall of the city as due to the work of one great foe (2:4). Furthermore, there is no suggestion of a schism in the realm of Assyria in Nahum's description; the attack is rather from an outside foe. Nor, indeed, was the situation of Nineveh at any time during the revolt so precarious as to warrant such a confident expectation of her destruction as Nahum entertains. Babylon in that revolt was not so intent upon destroying Nineveh and Assyria as upon gaining her own

independence from or even domination over Assyria. Then, too, if Nahum had had this revolt in mind, he would have hardly anticipated the destruction of Nineveh so vividly. He would have been much more likely to have conceived of Nineveh as becoming the capital of the new Babylonian power and his threats of destruction would have been confined to the dynasty reigning in Nineveh.[16]

6. This leaves us with the final suggestion of about 654 BC for the date of Nahum. Several things incline us toward this date. (1) Israel was very much under the burden of Assyrian oppression at this time, with no visible hope of escaping it. Perhaps Nahum's prophecy was intended to give Judah the hope they had lost in the circumstances pressing in upon them. (2) The fall of Thebes would still be fresh to all who read the prophecy. A pointed reference to it would have had a great impact at this time. (3) Assyria around 654 BC better fits the description of Nahum 3:1, 4, 16 (see above) than it does at later times, as the following inscription from the reign of Ashurbanipal indicates:

(5) Their tongues I pulled out, their overthrow I accomplished. (6) The rest of the people alive among the stone lions and bulls (7) which Sennacherib the grandfather of my begetter, in the midst had thrown; (8) again I in that pit, those men (9) in the midst I threw. Their limbs cut off (10) I caused to be eaten by dogs, bears, eagles, (11) vultures, birds of heaven, and fishes of the deep... (65) ... their heads I cut off, their lips (66) I tore out, and for the inspection of the people of my country, I brought to Assyria.[17]

(4) A final argument for this date is the fact that Nahum very specifically lists names in his prophecy such as Thebes/No-Amon, Ethiopia, Egypt, Put and Lubim. One would expect, had he been writing when the Medes, Babylonians and Scythians were international powers, that they would also have been named. But on the Biblical view of prophecy as revelation -- not, strictly, as history written in advance -- the absence of these names is explained by the fact that Nahum wrote when these nations were not yet significant, and God did not choose to reveal the names of Nineveh's destroyers.

The Fulfillment of Nahum's Prophecy

Having established a date for the writing of Nahum which seems best able to explain the facts, we can now survey the prophetic material and see from geographic, historical and archaeological sources how accurate the prophet was.

Today, the remains of Nineveh consist of two mounds, both of which have been extensively excavated in the past century. Between these mounds flows the Khosr river, which winds through the city to join the Tigris river, on whose bank Nineveh was situated. In his archaeological excavation of Nineveh, Layard noted that Nineveh had been flooded.[18] Nahum also mentions flooding three times (1:8; 2:6, 8):

...but with an overwhelming flood he will make an end of Nineveh... The river gates are thrown open and the palace collapses... Nineveh is like a pool, and its water is draining away.

Layard, Rawlinson, and Thompson and Hitchinson independently give evidence that the city was burned.[19] Again, the prophet Nahum wrote of this (2:13; 3:13, 15):

"I am against you," declares the LORD Almighty. "I will burn up your chariots in smoke"... The gates of your land are wide open to your enemies; fire has consumed their bars... There the fire will devour you.

Many historical sources mention the fall of Nineveh in passing. Three major sources readily available are Herodotus, Diodorus and the *Babylonian Chronicle*. The basic account of the destruction is given by the last of these, with Herodotus providing corroboration. The enemy forces began their campaign against Nineveh by attacking the outlying areas in 614 BC. Some commentators feel that Nahum 3:12 refers to this: "All your fortresses are like fig trees with their first ripe fruit; when they are shaken, the figs fall into the mouth of the eater."

In 612, Nineveh itself was under siege for three summer months. Nahum also got this detail correct (3:14), with his reference to drawing water for the siege, unnecessary during the rainy season.

Although neither Herodotus nor the *Chronicle* refer to the flooding of the city, Diodorus does. In an interesting passage (some of which is admittedly inaccurate), Diodorus says that the flooding of the city was largely responsible for its defeat, as the river broke down a great length of wall on the northeast corner.

Sardanapallus, realizing that his entire kingdom was in the greatest danger... summoned forces and made preparations for the siege. Now there was a prophecy that had come down to him from his ancestors: "No enemy will ever take Ninus [Nineveh] by storm unless the river shall first become the city's enemy." Assuming, therefore, that this would never be, he held out in hope, his thought being to endure the siege and await the troops which would be sent by his subjects. The rebels, elated at their successes, pressed the siege, but because of the strength of the walls they were unable to do any harm to the men in the city... Consequently the siege dragged on, and for two years they pressed their attack, making assaults on the walls and preventing the inhabitants of the city from going out into the country; but in the third year, after there had been heavy and continuous rains, it came to pass that the Euphrates, running very full, both inundated a portion of the city and broke down the walls for a distance of twenty stades [2.5 miles].[20]

There are some discrepancies with the names -- Euphrates instead of Khosr or Tigris, and Sardanapallus for Sin-shar-ish-kun.   Even so, we have a fascinating account which seems to preserve a number of historical details. Further on, Diodorus speaks of rampant drunkenness at the time of the city's capture and a (possibly apocryphal) funeral pyre which the king built for himself and his court, that they might not be taken alive by the enemy.   There are many other points at which Nahum's prophecy parallels the record preserved in history and archaeology; an extensive listing is given by Walter Maier in his commentary. We give only one more here. Nahum 2:9-10 reads:

Plunder the silver! / Plunder the gold! / The supply is endless, / the wealth from all its treasures! / She [Nineveh] is pillaged, plundered, stripped!"

The *Babylonian Chronicles* say of Nineveh:

Kyaxares, King of Babylon, King of Umman-manda -- barbarian hordes [i.e., Scythians] -- from month of Sivan [June] to Av [August] they advanced with difficulty. They carried off much spoil and turned city into ruin-mound and heap of debris.[21]

Conclusions

From this brief survey we can see that the prophecy of Nahum is specific, complete and accurate, yet apparently written forty years before the events described, when the Assyrian empire was still all-powerful. Nineveh, the splendid capital of a mighty empire, was taken (as predicted) by siege, destroyed by fire and flood in summer, after its outer fortifications had been picked off one by one.

Some, of course, will not be impressed by *any* arguments for the date of Nahum if these result in his description of the fall of Nineveh being really predictive. But there is one point from which we *cannot* escape, the thorough and lasting destruction of the city. Nahum says (1:12): "Although they have allies and are numerous, they will be cut off and pass away." In 1:14, he says:

The LORD has given a command concerning you, Nineveh, "You will have no descendants to bear your name.... I will prepare your grave, for you are vile."

And in 3:18-19:

O king of Assyria, your shepherds slumber; / your nobles lie down to rest. / Your people are scattered on the mountains / with no one to gather them. / Nothing can heal your wound; / your injury is fatal. / Everyone who hears the news about you / claps his hands at your fall, / for who has not felt your endless cruelty?

Though some have claimed the area of Nineveh was later inhabited by intermittent villages and settlements, the fact remains that imperial Nineveh was destroyed and ruined forever. As the *Cambridge Ancient History* remarks: "The disappearance of the Assyrian people will always remain an unique and striking phenomenon in ancient history."[22]

Part Two

Prophecies about
Israel

Chapter 6

The Dispersion and Oppression of the Jews

Samuel H. Kellogg

The Jews are unique among the peoples of the world. The antiquity of their recorded history, over 3500 years, puts them in a class with the Chinese and Egyptians. The oldest European nations are young by comparison. Israel's days of independence were long gone before Socrates and Plato taught in Athens. When Rome was founded, the Jewish kingdom was far past its prime. Before the time of Homer, in the legendary days of the Trojan War, Israel was already at the height of its royal power.

Even more unusual is the fact that, though the Jews have existed as a people for so long, most of the time they were without political independence or even a national homeland. Even if we count the whole time from the exodus to the Babylonian conquest as a time of Israeli independence, we still find that the Jews have been under foreign government for three-fourths of their history. For half of their history, over eighteen hundred years, they have been scattered from their homeland into nearly every nation on earth.

Yet in all this time the Jews have not been assimilated so as to be lost to history, as so many of the neighboring peoples were. Nor have the Jews, for all these eighteen hundred years, had any land they could call their own, or any government to hold them together. In addition, they have suffered terrible persecution again and again, from the Romans in the first and second centuries, the Persians in the sixth, the Crusaders in the twelfth, Ferdinand and Isabella in the fifteenth, and culminating (so far) with Russia and Hitler in our own century. Nearly every influence which might obliterate a people has come upon the Jews over the centuries, as upon no other nation in history, and yet they still survive today.

No less striking is the enormous influence these people have had in world history. Until the last century they had never numbered over six million. Throughout their history they have been despised and hated by almost every nation. Yet in spite of this, they have exerted a greater influence on the world than almost any other nation. This fact is even more remarkable when we realize that, unlike most other nations, their influence grew as their political power faded. The Jewish kingdom began its steady decline with the death of Solomon. Yet it was not until the following centuries that the Jewish prophets wrote those works which have made such an impact on the ideals and morals of Western civilization. And even later, when Judea had sunk to an insignificant province of the

Roman Empire, out of this same people arose Jesus of Nazareth. His short career has undeniably proved, however one may explain it, to have been the turning point in human history.

As to the nature and extent of the influence of the Jews, more might be said.[1] Let us note only one point. As A. A. Hodge reminds us, the only monotheistic religions which have ever prevailed among men are historically connected with those Jewish writings collectively known as the Bible.[2] All the monotheism in the world today -- be it Jewish, Christian, Islamic or their offshoots -- has its source in the Jewish nation. So far as we can see, except for the Jews, the world today would have been without a faith (at least in the form of any organized religion) in the existence of one personal God, the Creator and Governor of the world. Whatever influence the belief in such a Being has had on the history and destiny of man, it is certainly a measure of the influence of the Jewish nation.

This fact, remarkable as it is, could not have been anticipated from anything in the Israeli gene pool or their early history. It is not a result of superior intelligence. While we fully recognize the endowments of the Jews in this area, there is no reason to believe they are above other races which could be named. It can hardly be attributed to their deeper spirituality, leading them more than others to seek God. In this respect, it is doubtful that they are naturally superior to races such as the Hindus. While rejecting all antisemitic connotations, it is not uncharitable to note that the Jews have never been noted for an otherworldly spirit.

Nor should we attribute Jewish monotheism to a "monotheistic genius" of the race, as Renan does. Archaeology has shown the early Semites were especially involved in idolatry and polytheism.[3] The Old Testament provides the same testimony for the Jews in particular. Despite all the instruction and warning provided by the prophets, the Jewish nation again and again turned to idolatry, including the cruelty of child sacrifice and the obscenities of fertility ritual. According to biblical history, this was the characteristic problem of the nation for the whole thirteen hundred years from the call of Abraham to the Babylonian captivity. No "monotheistic genius" here!

This combination of phenomena is unique in human history. It is not what one would expect in the ordinary course of events, but so exactly the reverse that many thinkers have felt it must be explained by supposing some supernatural power, working in some special, mysterious way in the history of the Jewish race.

Biblical Predictions about the Jews

In any case, these phenomena strongly underline yet another fact, which is more noteworthy than any of these. Among all the nations of the earth, the Jews alone have had their history written in advance. There is hardly a notable feature in their entire history, however improbable, that is not predicted with such detail in the Bible that it needs no correction, in spite of the large fraction of Israel's history which has occurred since the Bible was written.

This statement, by the way, is not particularly affected by any objections which liberal critics have raised about the date and authorship of the books which contain this prophetic history. Whether Deuteronomy, for instance, was written in the time of Moses or Josiah, it still contains an impressive summary of the most characteristic and exceptional events in Jewish history from then till now.[4]

These biblical predictions about Israel can be divided by subject matter into three categories: the people, the land, and the Holy City. Here we discuss only the first. These prophecies can also be categorized by result: disaster or prosperity. We here confine our attention to the disasters.

Predictions of disaster to come upon Israel are not only numerous, but also specific and detailed. They are not just general prophecies of calamity as could be safely predicted of any nation. On the contrary, they give us detailed and precise pictures of the various calamities and miseries to come upon Israel.

Furthermore, when we combine the various features of these prophecies into a single picture, they represent an experience which had, up to the time the predictions were given, never happened to any nation on earth. Yet, unlikely as it seemed in advance, these predictions have been so exactly fulfilled in the Jewish people that the language of the prophets often reads like history.

First of all, we have predictions that Israel would abandon the God who brought them out of Egypt and worship idols.

> When I have brought them into the land flowing with milk and honey, the land I promised on oath to their forefathers, and when they eat their fill and thrive, they will turn to other gods and worship them, rejecting me and breaking my covenant.... I know what they are disposed to do, even before I bring them into the land I promised them on oath (Deut 31:20-21).

How truly these words came to pass we learn from the biblical historians themselves. The abandonment of God's law was so universal that liberal critics have used this fact to argue that the Mosaic legislation could not have originated until after the exile. "How could the covenant and law have been so utterly ignored," they ask, "if it had been in existence at all?" This question has been answered by others,[5] and it would divert us from our present purpose to deal with it here. We only remark that, to the extent that the law was so abandoned, it impressively illustrates the fulfillment of a very improbable prediction.

It was also foretold that this apostasy would not be merely partial or superficial. Except for a "very small remnant," the whole nation would be characterized by blindness and hardness of heart. In most impressive language, God tells Isaiah that this would be the result of his ministry:

Go and tell this people, "Be ever hearing, but never understanding; be ever seeing, but never perceiving." Make the heart of this people calloused; make their ears dull and close their eyes. Otherwise they might see with their eyes, hear with their ears, understand with their hearts, and turn and be healed (Isa 6:9-10).

This prediction has been fulfilled in the Jewish nation on more than one occasion. Despite the warnings of their prophets, they stubbornly continued in idolatry till they were crushed by the Babylonian power. So blind were they that, when their promised Messiah came, as predicted by the prophets, they did not recognize him, but had him put to death as a blasphemer and troublemaker.[6] The words of the apostle Paul are as true today of the majority of the Jews as they were at his time:

Even to this day when Moses is read, a veil covers their hearts (2 Cor 3:15). Israel has experienced a hardening in part until the full number of the Gentiles has come in (Rom 11:25).

Furthermore, it was further predicted that, because of their sins, they would be subjected to their enemies, their cities besieged, and they themselves destroyed by sword, famine and disease. Centuries before these disasters occurred they were warned:

...if you reject my decrees... I will bring upon you sudden terror, wasting diseases and fever that will destroy your sight and drain away your life.... I will set my face against you so that you will be defeated by your enemies; those who hate you will rule over you.... When you withdraw into your cities, I will send a plague among you... When I cut off your supply of bread... they will dole out the bread by weight. You will eat, but you will not be satisfied (Lev 26:15-17, 25-26).

As the final result of all these calamities, it was predicted that the Jews would be taken from their own land and scattered into all the nations of the world. This threat is repeated again and again, with great emphasis. And such a scattering, please note, is hardly a necessary result of foreign domination. The Romans, for instance, to whom the last and most extensive scattering of the Jews is due, conquered many nations; generally they allowed these nations to remain in their own land if they would submit to Rome. But the biblical predictions of foreign conquest regularly indicate that Israel will not be allowed even this poor consolation. Instead they would be scattered among the nations and many would be sold into slavery:

The LORD will cause you to be defeated before your enemies. You will come at them from one direction but flee from them in seven, and you will become a thing of horror to all the kingdoms on earth.... You will be uprooted from the land you are entering to possess. Then the LORD will scatter you among all nations, from one end of the earth to the other (Deut 28:25, 63-64). Your sons and daughters will be given to another nation, and you will wear out your eyes watching for them day after day, powerless to lift a hand.... You will have sons and daughters but you will not keep them, because they will go into captivity (Deut 28:32, 41).

All this, however unlikely it may have seemed, has been fulfilled in detail. Again and again before the final overthrow of the Jewish state, Jerusalem and the other cities of Israel were besieged by foreign armies and experienced all the horrors of famine and disease, just as predicted. The Bible tells us how in the siege under Nebuchadnezzar "the children and infants faint" in the famine, saying to their mothers, "Where is bread and wine?" while "with their own hands compassionate women have cooked their own children" for food (Lam 2:11-12; 4:10). This experience was repeated on occasion as long as the Jews continued to inhabit the land.

For instance, under Antiochus Epiphanes (168 BC) during the fourteenth siege of Jerusalem, the city was pillaged, ten thousand captives taken, its walls destroyed, its finest buildings burned, the temple altar was defiled by the sacrifice of pigs, and the Jews were forbidden to practice their religion and cruelly tortured.[7]

The siege of Jerusalem under Titus (AD 70) is described by the eyewitness Josephus.[8] Crowded together in the city to celebrate Passover, the Jews were trapped by the siege, decimated by famine and disease, and killed by the sword in immense numbers, just as Jesus predicted (Luke 21:20-24). It is said that over one million died. Multitudes were carried away, either to be put to death as entertainment in the amphitheatres, or to drag out a miserable existence as slaves. So many were taken, the historian tells us, that the slavemarkets of the Roman Empire were glutted.[9] Such calamity has rarely happened to any nation, but even this was not the end.

In AD 116, the Jews revolted against Rome in North Africa, where large numbers had earlier been taken captive. The revolt was only suppressed again after multitudes of the miserable people had been put to death.

The Jews made a last attempt at regaining their national independence when they revolted against Rome under the leadership of Bar-Kochba in AD 132. This was put down three years later, after another bloody struggle in which nearly 600 thousand Jews died, often with frightful torture.[10] The survivors were again sold into grievous slavery and deported from the country. The Holy City was razed, and for two centuries no Jew was allowed within sight of the city (except for one day a year) on penalty of death. As Jesus said, "There will be great distress in the land and wrath against this people" (Luke 21:23). Did such a prediction ever come to pass with more terrible literality?[11]

Not only was this unusual scattering and exile of the whole nation predicted, but the prophets also give the most vivid and terrible picture of what the Jews would experience in this exile. For example, they would be always "oppressed and robbed":

... day after day you will be oppressed and robbed, with no one to rescue you.... The alien who lives among you will rise above you higher and higher, but you will sink lower and lower.... in hunger and thirst, in nakedness and dire poverty, you will serve the enemies the LORD sends against you (Deut 28:29, 43, 48).

In the presence of such misery and calamity, the Bible predicts that their former military courage will evaporate:

Among those nations you will find no repose, no resting place for the sole of your foot. There the LORD will give you an anxious mind, eyes weary with longing, and a despairing heart. You will live in constant suspense, filled with dread both night and day, never sure of your life. In the morning you will say, "If only it were evening!" and in the evening, "If only it were morning!" -- because of the terror that will fill your hearts and the sights that your eyes will see (Deut 28:65-67). As for those of you who are left, I will make their hearts so fearful in the lands of their enemies that the sound of a windblown leaf will put them to flight (Lev 26:36).

As to the duration of these fierce calamities, the Bible clearly predicts they will not be brief. On the contrary:

If you do not carefully follow all the words of this law... and do not revere this glorious and awesome name -- the LORD your God -- the LORD will send fearful plagues on you and your descendants, harsh and prolonged disasters, and severe and lingering illnesses (Deut 28:58-59).

History, indeed, testifies that the ancient prophets accurately described the experience of the Jewish nation. Their "disasters" were to be "harsh and prolonged." To date they have already continued for more than two thousand years. During this period, in one place or another, these words have been true of the Jewish people as of no other.

Under pagan Rome, their lot was hard; under Christian Rome it became harder still. Constantine, as soon as he came to power, began to take action against the Jews. They soon became, for all practical purposes, an outlawed people. Justinian, whose code came to form the basis for civil law throughout Europe, expressly excluded the Jews from the protections of his code. From then on, with local and temporary exceptions, the Jews became more and more the objects of the most irrational and pitiless hatred ever directed against any people.

Again and again the fury of the people was stirred up against them by slanderous accusations of atrocious crimes. Nothing was too bad to be believed of a Jew. They were charged with black magic; with stealing the wafer used in the Lord's supper to insult it in their synagogues; with celebrating the passover using the blood of Christian children whom they had kidnapped, tortured and crucified for this purpose. The effect of such slander is not surprising. Throughout Europe the Jews regularly experienced confiscation of property, violence, torture, massacre, banishment, and all sorts of ingenious and systematic insults. The Crusades, especially, began the darkest hour of terror for the Jews. This gloom lasted, with only occasional brightening, for many centuries. Gibbon tells us:

> The mad enthusiasts of the first crusade found their first and most easy warfare against the Jews, the murderers of the Son of God. In the trading cities of the Moselle and the Rhine, their colonies were numerous and rich; and they enjoyed, under the protection of the emperor, the free exercise of their religion. At Verdun, Spires, Treves, Mentz, Worms, many thousands were pillaged and massacred; nor had they felt a more bloody stroke since the persecution of Hadrian [AD 135]. A remnant was saved by the firmness of their bishops, who accepted a feigned and transient conversion; but the more obstinate Jews opposed their fanaticism to the fanaticism of the Christians, barricaded their houses, and precipitating themselves, their families and their wealth into the rivers or the flames, disappointed the malice, or at least the avarice, of their implacable foes.[12]

From then on the Jews of Europe existed only to be plundered. In the German states they were considered slaves of the emperor. If in any state they enjoyed a brief toleration, the privilege was purchased at the cost of enormous taxation. In any case, oppression and plunder was the rule. Sometimes it was at the hands of brutal mobs, stirred up by fanatic priests. At other times -- in a more formal way and on a larger scale -- by the "most Christian" kings of Europe, who followed the fashion of the times in plundering, banishing, torturing and killing Jews as it chanced to please them, all in the name of Christ and law! In 1290 they were expelled from England, and were not allowed to return from nearly four hundred years. In 1395 they were expelled from France. And in 1492, at the instigation of the inquisitor Torquemada, they were forced from Spain, where they had for several centuries enjoyed an unusual degree of peace and prosperity. This expulsion was especially marked by cruelty and atrocities.

So it continued for the first half of our present millennium. With the Reformation, the severity of such persecution was reduced as the power of the papacy declined. Yet with a few exceptions, the Protestant princes of Europe showed little more willingness than their Catholic predecessors to accord the Jews the common rights of man. In many countries they were not allowed to live at all. Where they were tolerated, they still had to submit to all sorts of indignities, insults and oppressions, both from rulers and people. In many places, as in Russia and Nazi Germany in our century, they had to wear peculiar clothing or distinguishing badges. By law they had to live in certain cramped and unhealthy parts of the cities, from whence our term "ghettos." They had to be indoors by early evening. On days of church festivals, they were often required to stay indoors. Throughout much of Europe, the Jew had to pay a tax whenever he crossed a border between the many small states into which Europe was then divided. In parts of France, he had to pay the same toll as a donkey any time he passed through a gate or crossed a bridge. In most countries Jews were prohibited from owning land. They were excluded from all universities and colleges, and from almost every occupation that was considered honorable. Whatever they succeeded in earning under such restrictions, the governments of Europe continually devised new ways to rob them of it under the forms of Christian law.

Such was the history of the Jews from the destruction of Jerusalem down to about 1800. With the rise of secularism, it looked for a while as though they would at last be treated as equals. Yet again and again, with the rise of Naziism, Communist antisemitism, and Islamic opposition to the state of Israel, the same phenomena of Jewish mistreatment have continued to recur. Could event correspond to prediction any more precisely than the history of the Jews has so far? "The LORD will send... harsh and prolonged disasters... you will have nothing but cruel oppression all your days" (Deut 28:59, 33). How true it has proved!

As a result of such calamities, Israel was further told they would become few in number:

You who were as numerous as the stars in the sky will be left few in number, because you did not obey the LORD your God (Deut 28:62).

Like all the rest, this prediction has been fulfilled also. Basnage estimated, at the beginning of the eighteenth century, that the world Jewish population, which during the kingdom period may have been as high as seven or eight million, was then no more than three million.[13] No doubt it is much greater now. But the Nazi holocaust wiped out about six million Jews according to the best estimates, about two-thirds the Jewish population of Europe at that time.[14]

Such then has been the lot of the Jewish people for centuries. No other nation has ever existed of which such experiences are recorded. As a result, the Jew has become precisely what the prophet said he would become, "a thing of horror, and an object of scorn and ridicule to all the nations where the LORD will drive you" (Deut 28:37). The very word "Jew" has become a term of contempt. The name of this people, to whom God's revelation and His Messiah came, came to be used, as when people speak of "jewing" a person, as a synonym of all that is base in character and dishonorable in business.

Other predictions concerning the long tribulation of the nation might be added, all of which have been similarly fulfilled. Ezekiel for instance, predicting the fall of the throne of Judah, declared that the crown of the house of David would not be restored again during the time of Israel's abasement:

O profane and wicked prince of Israel, whose day has come, whose time of punishment has reached its climax, this is what the Sovereign LORD says: Take off the turban, remove the crown. It will not be as it was: The lowly will be exalted and the exalted will be brought low. A ruin! A ruin! I will make it a ruin! It will not be restored until he comes to whom it rightfully belongs; to him I will give it (Ezk 21:25-27).

So it has been. The attempts made to restore the kingdom since its fall in 587 BC have only by their failure made the fulfillment of the ancient prophecy more conspicuous. True, a kingdom was briefly established by the Maccabees at Jerusalem in the second century BC, but the kings were not of the royal house of David, nor even of the royal tribe of Judah. The Herods ruled briefly in the first century BC and the first AD, but their lineage was no better than the Maccabees'. And now for nearly two thousand years no one of any tribe of Israel has borne the title of king over the Jewish nation in Jerusalem. Like Ezekiel, Hosea too had said that the sons of Israel "will live for many days without king or prince" (Hos 3:4), and so it has come to pass.

In addition to all this, the prophets foretold that the privileges of God's grace which the Jews had abused would be taken away and, during the whole time of their rejection, given to others. Hosea speaks of a time when God would say to Israel, "You are not my people, and I am not your God" (Hos 1:9). Similarly, Jesus told the Jews: "Therefore I tell you that the kingdom of God will be taken away from you and given to a people who will produce its fruit" (Matt 21:43).

To these predictions of the spiritual condition of Israel during the time of their rejection, Hosea adds a remarkable prediction that, while Israel would be cured at last of idolatry, they would yet remain a long time without the particular religious practices God gave them at Sinai: "For the Israelites will live many days without king or prince, without sacrifice or sacred stones, without ephod or idol" (Hos 3:4).

No words could more succinctly describe the condition of Israel during this long period without a king. From the days of the return from Babylonian exile to the present, they have been without the idolatry and sacred stones which had proved such a temptation while they lived with the Canaanites in Palestine. The judgment of Babylonian exile pretty well ended idolatry among the Jews. But, in addition, it is also true that, since the first century AD, they have had neither the ephod (one of the priestly garments) nor sacrifice. Thus the ancient sacrificial ritual, commanded by God at Sinai as the central part of Jewish worship, has ceased, just as

Hosea predicted. For nearly two thousand years, the Jews have been without their Sinai religion, yet without idolatry! Could any more striking characterization of Israel's history be made?

We need not further multiply illustrations. It is a historical fact that the disaster predicted to come upon Israel has been fulfilled in detail.

Conclusions

To sum up what we have said, the ancient predictions of the Bible regarding the Jewish nation have been fulfilled with a degree of literality almost equivalent to having had their history written in advance. Such a phenomenon is to be met with nowhere outside this nation and the Scriptures which originated among them. This phenomenon, added to all else which is so unique and peculiar in this people, rightly demands the most earnest and thoughtful consideration of everyone.

It is true that other books, both Jewish and Gentile, sometimes contain what profess to be predictions of the future. Such cases, upon closer examination, prove to have little in common with the prophecies of the Bible. In many instances, subsequent history contains nothing corresponding to the event predicted. In other cases, the predictions are so vague and general that their fulfillment is not surprising. Still others bear distinct traces of having been written after the events foretold, or so immediately in advance of the events that they may be easily explained as forecasts by shrewd minds.

The predictions here discussed are *quite different*. They are scattered through a collection of writings produced among this one Jewish people, and no other, during a period of about 1500 years. In many instances they refer to nothing immediately impending, such as might have been anticipated by natural reason. Rather, they deal with a series of events reaching so far into the future that we, who live 1900 years after the last predictions were made, have not yet seen the end of their fulfillment. We can therefore rule out the possibility that they are all prophecies made after the event.

Nor should we omit the observation made earlier that the essential facts which bear on this matter are not affected by any questions raised by modern criticism on the dates of the various books which contain the predictions. Let every book be dated at the latest dates claimed by radical criticism (165 BC for the Old Testament; AD 135 for the New). However the real predictive nature of some prophecies might be affected, we would still have a large remainder of true prophecies which were fulfilled only long after these dates.

The predictions given above make it most unlikely that these are only lucky guesses. Many of the events and circumstances foretold are just the *opposite* of what would have naturally occurred to patriotic Israelites, seeking to forecast their nation's future. Natural pride and patriotism would have produced a very different picture. These predictions were so offensive to the pride and contrary to the traditional religious attitudes of the people that they were almost unanimously disbelieved. For making such forecasts, the prophets were usually persecuted and sometimes killed (see, e.g., Jer 7:4; Ezk 11:2-3; Mic 3:11).

Moreover, many of these predictions were so *highly improbable* in themselves that no one desiring a reputation as a prophet could risk making them. Babylon, for example (or Assyria), was in the fulness of her strength, the mistress of the ancient world. Little Israel struggled in vain against her mighty power. Yet the prophets said Babylon would soon pass away, completely and forever. Israel, however, though she would go into a long captivity and suffer miseries for generations such as no other nation had; though she would be scattered among all nations, without a king, a country, a temple, or a priesthood to bind her together; yet she should never perish, never mingle with the nations or lose her distinctive identity. Was this such a forecast that unaided human intellect would devise as a probable anticipation of the future? Yet it was predicted and stands undeniably fulfilled before our eyes today!

Hosea gives us another no less striking illustration. He foretold that Israel would live many days without idolatry, priesthood or sacrifice. That he should anticipate that his people, as a result of God's corrective judgment, would finally be cured of their tendency to idol worship, is not unreasonable in view of the blessings planned for God's people in the end. But how *completely unlikely* it is that he would have ventured to predict that this long period without idolatry would also be characterized by the non-existence of the priesthood and the cessation of the Mosaic sacrifices, the only form of worship with which he was familiar or which was permitted to the nation!

The conclusion from all this is as clear and inescapable as it is important. Here is a nation whose whole history from its beginning has been unique in character; a people who, arising out of a race and age notable in the ancient world for the grossness of its idolatries, have yet been the undoubted source of all the monotheistic religion on the face of the earth; a people who, without those outward and visible cords of a common government and homeland, subjected for centuries to circumstances which should naturally have resulted in their extinction, have not only still survived, but have maintained a national life and a separateness from the many nations among which they have lived as has no other nation in history. As Cristlieb says, "the people of Israel [are] a perennial, living historical miracle"[15]

But the *strangest fact* of all remains. This same peculiar people has a literature, admittedly very ancient, in which all this unique experience is predicted, written out centuries before it even seemed possible. Is this all of no significance? Do these unparalleled phenomena in the history of Israel mean nothing? Can they reasonably be explained on purely naturalistic grounds? Have we here nothing but the wonderful Jewish "intuition"? Is there not the strongest reason to suspect the presence in this history and in these prophecies an element which is *not* of man, but from *above* man?

And when we observe that these prophets *expressly claim* that this was indeed the case; that under every pressure to the contrary, even when facing imprisonment and death because of the words they spoke, they still never wavered in the persistent assertion that the words they spoke were *not* their own words, but God's words, are we not compelled, as reasonable people, in the light of 2000 years of unbroken fulfillment of this prophetic history, to admit their claim and confess that, in a sense which is true of the words of no other men, the words of Jesus, the apostles and the prophets are indeed words of the living and omniscient God; and that the books in which these words are found, and of which they form an integral part, are indeed the very Word of God, and are therefore to be believed and obeyed accordingly? Can any reasonable and unbiased person escape this conclusion?

Another conclusion follows from this same line of argument. If these books are proven to be the Word of God by the occurrence of real prediction in them, then the conclusions of the modern radical schools of criticism against their genuineness and authenticity *cannot* be correct. There must somewhere be a flaw in the arguments by which such conclusions were reached. The prophetic element is woven into the very texture of these books; it cannot be removed without destroying the whole. If there is such a prophetic element in any book, then the book must be supernaturally inspired by God. Yet we are asked to believe that certain works professing to be written by Moses, Isaiah, or Daniel, for instance, were not really written by him, but by another centuries later, who, to give his book greater authority, published it in the name of an ancient worthy and palmed it off as such on his credulous fellow Jews! If such critics are right, we have here nothing less than *a God-inspired forgery*! Is such a thing a moral possibility?

Frederick the Great once asked a Christian clergyman to give him a brief and conclusive argument for the truth of Christianity. The minister promptly responded, "The Jews, your majesty!" The world, with all its claim to sophistication, has not yet outgrown that argument, though it has frequently neglected it. We suggest that the argument is, if anything, of greater force today than ever before.

Chapter 7

Hosea's Prophetic History of the Jews

John A. Bloom

In the eighth century BC the prophet Hosea portrayed the future of the Jewish people in terms of six prominent sociological features. These have been fulfilled in a most unusual way in the centuries following AD 70, extending down even to our own generation. This prophecy, unfortunately, has often been obscured by mistranslation or allegorical interpretation, and its validity has been attacked by liberal critics. Yet the clarity of the prophecy becomes apparent when we note the analogy it provides in the relation of Hosea and his wife Gomer to that of God and Israel.

The early chapters of Hosea contain the most striking *acted parable* in the Old Testament. Among the Jewish prophets, an acted parable was a means by which they would vividly illustrate their teaching, employing some unusual action to make their point allegorically or symbolically. Jeremiah, for instance, portrays the sudden and irreparable disaster to come upon Jerusalem by smashing a clay pot (Jer 19). Ezekiel eats rationed, low-quality bread to picture the siege-famine that Jerusalem would soon endure (Ezk 4:9-17).

In the case of Hosea, God commanded the prophet to marry Gomer, a woman apparently known to be unfaithful (1:2). They have several children, and then Gomer abandons Hosea for a less restrictive lifestyle (2:2-7). In chapter three, Hosea is commanded to renew his relationship to Gomer, so that the whole Hosea-Gomer relationship becomes a picture of God's continuing love toward Israel in spite of the nation's unfaithfulness to Him. Surprisingly, the main point in this model of God's future relation to Israel is not the renewal of conjugal relations. Instead, we find Hosea establishing a "many day" period of isolation, during which Gomer is to have no relations with any man, not even her own husband. This isolation is the predictive symbolism for God's dealings with wayward Israel: she, too, will be isolated, not only from self-chosen kings and idolatrous practices, but also from God-given kings and divinely established forms of worship. Yet this quarantine will not last forever; Hosea looks forward to God's eventual reestablishment of full relations with Israel (3:5).

Such is the impression given by a straight-forward reading of Hosea 3 in a Bible translation made by conservatives. Some modern writers, however, rejecting the possibility of supernatural prediction, try to set aside its predictive elements. Let us examine some of the literary-critical arguments raised against this prophecy and the interpretive problems involved in testing its fulfillment. First we shall consider the reliability of the original text. Then we will survey the grammatical, historical and interpretive matters which may affect our understanding of the passage, concentrating on textual parallelisms and the particular words which describe the predicted status of Israel. Finally, we give a brief overview of Israel's history, comparing it with various fulfillment schemes.

The Text of Hosea 3

The present Hebrew text of Hosea is generally recognized as one of the less well-preserved among Old Testament books.[1] Nevertheless, no serious textual problems occur within chapter three itself. A few differences between the Greek Septuagint and the Hebrew Masoretic texts are of interest; we will note these as we proceed.

Despite the manuscript evidence for the integrity of chapter three, liberal critics sometimes claim it has been tampered with. R. E. Clements, for example, believes Hos 3:5 is "spurious without question" because it refers to the Davidic dynasty of Judah.[2] The purpose of Hosea, he claims, "was to forewarn the people of a coming period of chastisement and deprivation... not to demonstrate the enduring nature of Yahweh's love for Israel."[3] In Clements' view, 3:5 is the work of a later editor, whose "clear endeavor [was] to elaborate a message of hope on the basis of prophecies which were originally threatening in character."[4]

Such a glib rejection of Hosea's references to Messiah and to Judah has been contested even by other liberal scholars. They note that "when each passage is studied independently, on the basis of relevance of context and literary form, the authenticity of most of the references to Judah becomes clear."[5] Gordis suggests "the literary prophets look forward to a reunited Hebrew nation."[6] Anderson and Freedman feel there is no reason to reject 3:5 as an interpolation since "the thought is not inconsistent with prophetic views generally, and there is need for a suitable conclusion to the section." "We hardly know enough about Hosea's political thinking," they continue, "to rule out the restoration of the Davidic kingdom as an eschatological expectation."[7]

As there is no evidence within the context that 3:5 is an editorial addition, we will interpret the chapter as it stands.

Interpretation of Hosea 3

For the purposes of our discussion, we propose the following as a reasonable, literal English translation:

(1) Then the LORD said to me, "Go again, love a women who is loved by her husband, yet an adulteress, even as the LORD loves the sons of Israel, though they turn to other gods and

love raisin cakes."

(2) So I procured her for myself for fifteen shekels of silver and a homer and a lethech of barley.

(3) Then I said to her, "You shall stay with me for many days. You shall not play the harlot, nor shall you have a man; then indeed I will be yours."

(4) For the sons of Israel will remain for many days without king and without prince and without sacrifice and without cult pillar and without ephod and teraphim.

(5) Afterward the sons of Israel will return and seek the LORD their God and David their king; and they will come trembling to the LORD and to His goodness in the last days.

This translation parallels that of the *New American Standard Bible* except as follows: "procured" is substituted for "bought" (v 2); "lethech" replaces "half" (2); and "then indeed I will be yours"[8] takes the place of "so I will also be toward you" (3). Verse 4 follows the literal Hebrew, as the precise phrasing is important for our later discussion.

Some Specific Words

Husband is the preferred translation of the Hebrew *reach* (pronounced rey-ack) in Hos 3:1. Although it occurs 187 times in the OT and is often translated "friend, companion, another person,"[9] most of these are discussing relations between men. Only three passages, besides our own, involve an obvious male-female relationship:

Surely, as a woman treacherously departs from her *lover*, so you have dealt treacherously with Me, O house of Israel (Jer 3:20).

... but you are a harlot with many *lovers*... (Jer 3:1).

... she has none to comfort her among all her *lovers* (Lam 1:2).

Jer 3:1 and Lam 1:2 both refer to illicit relationships, but Jer 3:20 fits most naturally within the context of a marriage commitment. Thus, in addition to the general term "friend", *reach* may be rendered either "illicit lover" or "husband" for a male-female context.

The "illicit lover"[10] possibility has sparked the imagination of many scholars, as it could imply that Hosea was commanded to love someone other than Gomer.[11] However, such a view ignores the explicit parallelism in Hos 3:1 between the "woman who is loved by a *reach*" and the Israelites who are loved by the LORD. The LORD is never pictured as an illicit lover of Israel but as the faithful husband of an immoral wife (cp Ezk 16).

Translating *reach* neutrally as "another" (as in the *Anchor Bible* and NEB) may capture the range of the word's meaning, but such ambiguity in English brings in an illicit connotation that strains the parallelism noted above. So although "husband" is an unusual translation for *reach*, it is preferred in this passage because the context rules out any immoral sense. The *reach* is the woman's rightful lover. God is here instructing Hosea to love Gomer again in spite of her adultery, since God continues to love Israel despite her spiritual adultery.[12]

Procured in 3:2 is probably derived from a Hebrew verb meaning "to buy," though its form is unusual. We translate following the suggestion of the *Anchor Bible*[13] rather than the KJV "bought," since the latter adds a connotation of slavery. This has led to the assumption that Gomer, as a result of her sin, has sunk to the level of slavery, and Hosea is graciously redeeming her from her taskmasters.[14] The text gives no warrant for this idea, especially as the phrase "for myself" immediately follows the verb. If the slavery picture is at all correct, Hosea is purchasing Gomer to be his personal slave, not buying her freedom.

To avoid this erroneous connotation, our translation follows Nyberg's preference[15] for the sense "to hire," in agreement with the Greek Septuagint version. This rendering, however, implies that Hosea is "hiring" a harlot for himself. Moral objections have been raised against this idea, even if the harlot is understood to be Hosea's own wife Gomer. Gordis notes: "The ancient Hebrew horror of adultery went beyond the guilty parties and forbade the husband to continue to live with his faithless wife."[16] But it is unwise to reject this rendering because it suggests a repugnant and technically "illegal" situation. God is using the Hosea-Gomer relationship to picture both the atrocity of Israel's sin and the greatness of His love and forgiveness. We should not fault Hosea for obeying God's command (3:1) and renewing his relationship with his physically adulterous wife unless we are also prepared to castigate God for His more serious "sin" of renewing relationship with His spiritually adulterous people Israel.

That Hosea needed to hire Gomer in order to renew his relation with her implies that she was still unrepentant and could only be "tricked" into living with Hosea through one of her customary business deals. Apparently the price of 15 shekels and a homer and lethech of barley was sufficient to purchase her services for "many days."

King (v 4) obviously refers to the political leader of the nation. Whether this term should be restricted to members of the Davidic dynasty or include the kings of the apostate Northern Kingdom cannot be determined from the general usage of the word. Nyberg takes "king and prince" in a wholly religious sense, claiming this reference "is not to the political leaders, but to the god Melek (or Malik) and the lower deities who were members of the heavenly court."[17] Such a view, however, ignores the obvious political sense of "king" and "prince" elsewhere in Hosea (5:1,10; 8:4; and 13:10-11).

Prince occurs 381 times in the OT with a broad range of meaning. Its basic significance is "leader" or "official" but this may be used in political, military, religious or other senses.[18] Its occurrence in conjunction with "king" elsewhere in Hosea suggests a political application here.

Sacrifice clearly refers to Israel's worship and religion. Whether Hosea has in mind the Mosaic temple offerings or the paganizing practices then rampant in Israel cannot be answered from the meaning of the word itself.

Pillar also displays a range of meaning in the OT. In patriarchal times, it referred to a monument, such as that at Rachel's grave (Gen 35:20). By Hosea's time, pillars were frequently associated with idolatrous pagan worship: "For they also built for themselves high places and *pillars* and Asherim on every high hill and beneath every luxuriant tree" (1 Kings 14:23). Even patriarchal sites like Bethel had been corrupted. The Septuagint has "altar" here instead of "pillar," which may indicate a textual variant going back to the Hebrew.

Ephod usually refers to the Mosaic ephod, one of the garments of the high priest. The Septuagint follows this understanding, paraphrasing "ephod" by "priesthood," apparently taking the former to be a synecdoche for the latter, i.e., a figure in which a part stands for the whole. However, ephods were also used in corrupted forms of Israelite worship; recall the ephods of Gideon (Judges 8) and Micah (Judges 17-18). Liberal commentaries often define the ephod as "an image of the deity"[19] by citing the corrupt cultic practices and ignoring the Pentateuchal use of the term. But wherever we can test its usage, the ephod is a *garment* of some sort. An assumption of pagan meaning here unnecessarily restricts the interpretation of our passage.

In the absence of any clear Biblical evidence that ephods were used in the religion of the Northern Kingdom, Hosea is more likely speaking of the true ephod worn by the high priest in Jerusalem. This ephod had a pocket in which to carry the *Urim and Thummim*, a device of some sort for consulting God (1 Sam 23:9-12). In our discussion below, we will consider both the literal and figurative interpretations of "ephod."

Teraphim refers to household idols. The Nuzi texts have shown that during the patriarchal period these were used to indicate leadership over the family.[20] They had no part in the Mosaic regulations for worship, but seem to have been used for divination in pagan circles (Ezk 21:21; Zech 10:2). The Septuagint translation "manifestations" probably indicates that knowledge of the meaning of *teraphim* had been lost by about 200 BC.

Sons of Israel occurs three times in our chapter as the subject of the prophecy. Thus we need to consider carefully how the phrase is to be understood.

The term "Israel" is used in Scripture *both* for the whole Israelite nation and for the Northern Kingdom in particular. For the Northern Kingdom the alternative term "Ephraim" is frequently used, a synecdoche in which the dominant tribe of the ten northern tribes stands for the whole group, just as "Judah" is commonly used to indicate the Southern

Kingdom. There is no comparable alternate term for the whole Israelite people.

The prophet Hosea is clearly directing his message primarily to the Northern Kingdom. The majority of occurrences of "Israel" in Hosea refer to this kingdom, as is clear from contexts in which we have contrasts with Judah (Hos 1:1,6,11; 4:15; etc.), parallelisms with Ephraim (8:8; 9:1; 10:6; 11:8; 14:1; etc.), references to the house of Jehu (1:4), setting up kings without God's consent (8:3), and localities in the Northern Kingdom (5:1; 8:6).

Yet Hosea contains passages where Israel is mentioned in a context with both Ephraim and Judah (5:5,9; 11:12), for which a general term referring to both groups taken together would not be unreasonable. We also find references to the exodus of Israel out of Egypt (3:1; 11:1; 12:13), which are more appropriate to the nation as a whole. Two references to the "days of Gibeah" as a time of great sin for Israel (9:9 and 10:9) make better sense as referring to the whole nation, since it was the tribe of Benjamin, a part of the Southern Kingdom, that was the culprit in this affair (Judges 19-21).

Thus the "sons of Israel" could refer to the Israelite people as a whole or to the northern tribes in particular. We will need to consider both possibilities in our survey of historical evidence of fulfillment.

Parallelisms within the Passage

Hosea chapter 3, in its very nature as an acted prophecy, is sprinkled with parallels relating to the Hosea-Gomer/God-Israel analogy. The most obvious one is the statement that, as Gomer is to remain "for many days" without any conjugal relations and then she will be reinstated with her husband (v 3), so the sons of Israel will remain "for many days" in their prophesied condition (v 4) and then be reinstated with the LORD (v 5).

At the time of Hosea, the Northern Kingdom had abandoned the LORD in two areas. (1) Politically she had seceded from the Davidic monarchy.[21] (2) Religiously she had developed her own cult in order to be independent of the Jerusalem temple. As a further corruption, she had also turned to the Canaanite Baal worship. Paralleling the manner in which the rebellious Gomer was isolated from both improper and proper conjugal relationships in the area of her rebellion (marriage), so the sons of Israel are to be isolated from both improper and proper relationships to God in the areas of their rebellion, both political and religious (v 4).

The "without" list of v 4 (king, prince, sacrifice, pillar, ephod and teraphim) can be understood in two different ways: (1) taking all the items to be descriptive of Israel's rebellious condition, with Israel's proper state (Davidic kingship and temple worship) not specified;[22] or (2) considering the list to be composed of items from both the proper and rebellious state, organized in "neither/nor" pairs.

The first alternative (all rebellious) requires only that the item "ephod" be understood in an *idolatrous* rather than orthodox sense. The Judges 17-18 incident regarding Micah's shrine gives sufficient Scriptural warrant for this, particularly as this incident seems to lie behind the later choice of Dan as one of the two main Northern Kingdom shrines. The other five items are either clearly pagan (e.g., "teraphim") or general enough (e.g., "sacrifice") to fit this model. The grammar of v 4 favors this approach, as each of the six items are listed using "without" except for the last ("without ephod and teraphim"). Such an omission typically serves in Hebrew as an end-of-list marker. The redundant "and without" for all items but the last closely parallels the use of "from" in the list of cities in 2 Kings 17:24: "from Babylon and from Cuthah and from Avva and from Hamath and Sepharvaim." Note that the last city does not have "from" with it, thereby marking the end of the list.

The weakness of this "all rebellious" scheme is that no explicit fulfillment is given for the *second aspect* of Hosea's acted prophecy -- the delay in reinstatement of conjugal relations. Thus the parallelism between Hosea and God is not fully worked out. If there is no direct reference to orthodox worship in this list, then this prophecy only states that Israel will abandon pagan worship, and an immediate return to Mosaic worship would be expected. But in that case, the statement in v 5 concerning Israel's return in the last days makes little sense.[23]

Alternative (2), a "neither/nor" list, *preserves* the parallelism between the parable and its specified fulfilment. However, we might expect greater contrast between the paired items than is evident, particularly between "king" and "prince." Within this alternative, we could understand "king" to refer to the Davidic dynasty and "prince" to non-Davidic rulers such as the Northern Kingdom had in Hosea's time.

The pairs do divide nicely into three distinct areas: political (king and prince), religious ritual (sacrifice and pillar) and religious divination (ephod and teraphim). Notice that, within these pairs, the first item of each appears to have Old Testament approval: (Davidic) kingship, (Mosaic) sacrifice and the (Levitical) ephod. The second item of each could be understood as having a rebellious origin: princes (who revolted against the Southern Kingdom), (Canaanite) pillars, and teraphim. But word studies alone cannot confirm these connotations, since three of them (king, prince and sacrifice) have broad ranges of meaning. However, an isolation from both God-approved and rebellious elements in Israel's socio-religious relation with God best fits the parallel with the isolation Hosea imposed on Gomer.

A parallelism between the phrases of verse 5 should also be mentioned. "Afterward the sons of Israel will return and seek the LORD their God and David their king; and they will come trembling to the LORD and to His goodness in the last days." Whether this parallel is synonymous (repetitive) or synthetic (second element building on first) will depend on how we handle verse 5a. If we *split* "return" and "seek," then we may deduce that a return to the land will precede a return to God, and that the second half of the verse adds to the first. If we *lump* the two verbs "return" and "seek," then the second half virtually repeats the first. Since we learn elsewhere that Israel's return to her homeland in the last days will be unique in that she will still be unrepentant (see Ezk 36:24-31; Zech 12:10-13:1; 13:8-9; 14:21; and Rev 11:1-13), we need not argue over Hos 3:5. It is most reasonable to conclude that it predicts both a return to the land and to God, but the state of the returning people is not specified. A nonrepentant return should be considered only a preliminary fulfillment.

The Fulfillment of Hosea 3

Armed with an understanding of the text, we now turn to the records of history to discuss the fulfillment of this prophecy. Basic to any analysis of fulfillment must be the question:

To Whom Does the Prophecy Apply?

As noted above, the prophecy is explicitly directed to the "sons of Israel," who could be either the whole Israelite nation or descendants of the Northern Kingdom tribes in particular. The dispersion of this latter group complicates our tracing of their history. Let us consider them first, calling them "Ephraim" for convenience.

The first major scattering of Ephraim occurred in 733-732 BC when the Assyrian king Tiglath-pileser III conquered Trans-Jordan and Galilee and "carried them captive to Assyria" (2 Kings 15:29). Modern Jewish historians doubt that this involved a complete depopulation of the region, feeling that "a considerable Israelite element remained, [since] it is not at all clear whether Galilee was resettled with foreign colonists."[24] Finegan, however, cites one of Tiglath-pileser's inscriptions concerning the fate of Israel: "Bit Humria [Israel] ... all its inhabitants I led to Assyria."[25] Finegan notes: "That such a ruthless deportation of people, doubtless in order to prevent future rebellions, was a usual feature of Tiglath-pileser's policy we know from other of his inscriptions."[26]

About 721 BC, the Assyrian king Sargon II conquered what remained of the Northern Kingdom. In his *Display Inscriptions*, Sargon boasts:

> I besieged and conquered Samaria, led away as booty 27,290 inhabitants of it. I formed from among them a contingent of 50 chariots and made the remaining inhabitants assume their social positions. I installed over them an officer of mine and imposed

upon them the tribute of the former king.[27]

According to the Bible, Ephraim was resettled "in Halah and Habor, on the river of Gozan, and in the cities of the Medes" (2 Kings 17:6). Sargon then "brought people from Babylon, Cuthah, Avva, Hamath and Sepharvaim and settled them in the towns of Samaria to replace the Israelites" (2 Kings 17:24). These imported people are "the kernel of what later became known as the Samaritans."[28] A clue to the extent of these deportations is found in the record of the great Passover which was celebrated in the eighteenth year of Josiah's reign. In attendance were "the priests, the Levites, all Judah and Israel who were present, and the inhabitants of Jerusalem" (2 Chron 35:18). Note also that when Josiah made repairs on the temple, he collected money "from Manasseh and Ephraim, and from all the remnant of Israel" (2 Chron 34:9). We may thus conclude that not all Ephraim was deported to Assyria, and that at least a fraction of those remaining were touched by Josiah's reform. While we have no explicit biblical or extra-biblical references to the fate of the *deported* Ephraimites, most modern scholars would agree with Ellison: "Sufficient of the Northern tribes joined Judah under the divided monarchy and doubtless at the return from exile to make the modern Jew representative of 'all Israel' (Rom 11:26)."[29]

By the time of the building of the second temple (515 BC), Ephraim had fragmented into three distinct groups: (1) those *exiled* by Assyria to Babylon, Cuthah, etc., known historically as "the ten lost tribes"; (2) those who *remained* in the land despite the exile, who apparently mixed with the imported gentiles to become the Samaritans; (3) Those who *merged* with Judah, having fled there during or after the fall of Samaria, or who joined the Judahites in exile. Each of these groups will be considered in the next section.

Our second possibility, that the term "sons of Israel" applies to the entire Israelite nation, can now be seen as an obvious deduction. Since a portion of Ephraim has mixed with the southern tribes to form the Israelites of later history, Hosea's prophecy should refer to the later nation as a whole, not only to any surviving splinter groups of isolated Ephraimites.

How Was This Prophecy Fulfilled?

The Ten Lost Tribes. The "ten lost tribes," as the name implies, are lost to history. They appear to have been killed off or assimilated into pagan races. According to H. Tadmor:

Little information is preserved about the ten tribes that were exiled to Assyria, whose fate was to serve later generations as a subject of legendary speculation and messianic hopes. What transpired was that most of those exiled were settled in the vicinity of Gozan on the Habor River.... Others were settled in

Media, where they apparently served as garrison troops in units organized with the Assyrian Army. This method of annexing into the Assyrian Army complete units from the armies of conquered peoples was widespread. Sargon, for instance, took fifty chariots from Samaria (or 200, according to another version), and added them to his royal guard; while Sennacherib absorbed Hezekiah's *elite* corps. This practice may help explain the presence in the Assyrian Army of an officer named Hilkiyau, i.e., Hilkiah, who is mentioned in a document from the time of Sargon recently discovered in Calah. Assyrian documents from Gozan itself also contain a few names that testify to the fact that an Israelite community still existed there in the seventh century. One document mentions two Gozan officials named Paltiyau and Niriyau. These, however, are scraps of information. It may be assumed that a part of the exiled tribes that still existed as a separate and conscious group in the days of Jeremiah and Ezekiel (see Jer 31:8 and Ezk 37:19-22) subsequently joined the exiles from Judah upon their return. The majority, however, were assimilated into the surrounding Aramean population, thus sharing the fate of every ethnic community displaced by the Assyrians and subjected to their policy of enforced Assyrianization. The spread of Aramaic as the lingua franca of the Assyrian Empire, especially in the west, hastened that process.[30]

From the fact that the majority of the "sons of Israel" were killed or assimilated into the gentile world's gene-pool, some might conclude that Hosea's prophecy was not fulfilled. But this is mistaken. The concept of the survival of a *remnant* is foundational to the prophetic literature, especially in passages of judgment. A particularly vivid example of this theme occurs in Ezekiel's "hair" prophecy concerning Jerusalem (Ezk 5).[31] That only a remnant of the "sons of Israel" would remain is suggested in Amos 5:15: "perhaps the LORD God of Hosts may be gracious to the remnant of Joseph."

Thus we need not grasp for fulfillment theories which find the "ten lost tribes" in the American Indians (as the Mormons do) or in modern Anglo-Americans (with the British-Israel movement). The assumption that God traces genealogies and will include in future fulfillments all those of remote Israelite descent is not necessary in light of His many assertions that only a remnant of Israel will survive.

The Samaritans. The Samaritans today are a recognized remnant of Ephraim.[32] Kelso goes so far as to state:

> Their history as recorded by Jewish sources describes Samaritans as descendants of the colonists whom the Assyrians planted in the Northern Kingdom, who intermarried with the Israelite population that the Assyrians had left in the land. More likely they were the pure descendants of the Israelites left in the

land, for Samaritan theology shows no sign of the influence of paganism among the colonists sent by the Assyrians. If there was intermarriage, the children became pure Israelites.[33]

While our knowledge of Samaritan history and religious practices is quite sketchy, such details as are readily available are summarized below.[34]

(1) *Political History.* Apparently the Samaritans were not involved in the Judahite exile following the fall of Jerusalem in 586 BC. One of our earliest political references to them is found in Ezra 4:2, where their request to join with Zerubbabel and the returning exiles in rebuilding the temple is refused. In Neh 2:10-6:14, strife is recorded between Nehemiah and the Samaritan governor Sanballat. A formal break finally occurred when the Samaritans built their own temple on Mount Gerizim about 332 BC. The bitter hostility seen in the New Testament accounts between Jews and Samaritans was the result of numerous hostile actions on both sides, culminating in the actions of Maccabean ruler John Hyrcanus, who subjugated the Samaritans and destroyed their temple in 129 BC.

Several features of Samaritan history parallel those of the Jews. Both groups suffered deportation to Egypt about 300 BC by Ptolemy Soter. Both joined in revolt against Roman rule in AD 66, with disastrous results. Both were persecuted by the Roman emperor Hadrian in the second century. Both were dispersed throughout the Roman empire, as Samaritans and their synagogues are known to have existed in ancient Egypt, Rome and other key regions.

Under the leadership of Baba Rabba in the fourth century AD, the Samaritans flourished briefly in their homeland. However, animosity with Christian groups soon led to persecution, and in 529 the emperor Justinian outlawed the sect. Under Arab and Turkish rule the Samaritans continued to experience almost constant oppression.

References to the Samaritans continue during medieval times. By the early seventeenth century, Samaritans had begun to move back to Nablus, near ancient Samaria and Shechem, from Damascus and elsewhere. As of 1970, about 430 Samaritans are known to survive, living in Nablus or in Tel Aviv.

(2) *Religious History.* Among the many interesting features of Samaritan religion we note the following. First, the cult is directed by a high priest, who originally traced his ancestry back to Aaron. However, this family line died out in 1623. Since then, the Samaritans have had what they call "Levite priests." At least in modern times, the high priest also acts as political leader. Second, the Samaritans today celebrate the Passover by means of an annual sacrifice on Mount Gerizim.

Samaritan fulfillment of Hosea 3 is a possibility we have not found discussed elsewhere. While many details of their history remain sketchy, the following points of corroboration may be noted.

(1) The Samaritans apparently have been without "king and prince,"

particularly in terms of homeland occupancy and leadership, from the persecutions of AD 529 to their return to the Nablus region in the seventeenth century. Their present situation, returned but without Aaronic priesthood, may be viewed as an initial fulfilment of verse 5.

(2) While a fulfilment in which sacrifice was completely absent would be ideal, the Samaritans have retained a form of the Passover ceremony. The relation of this rite to "sacrifice and pillar" is most interesting. (a) Mount Gerizim is not the proper location specified by the Bible for this sacrifice; thus it could not be considered orthodox if this is what Hosea meant by "sacrifice." In addition, a single annual sacrifice is an enormous reduction from the daily sacrifices prescribed in the Pentateuch. (b) The Passover ceremony is not a pagan rite; the Samaritans have abandoned the pillars associated with Canaanite religion. (c) Several times in their history the Samaritans have experienced such severe persecution as to be unable to celebrate this ceremony.

(3) The Samaritans are clearly "without ephod and teraphim." as they have turned from idolatry and have lost the Aaronic priesthood. Thus this phrase is fulfilled in the Samaritans even with a figurative interpretation of "ephod," not to mention the fact that the literal ephod is long gone.

In summary, the Samaritans are apparently a tiny remnant of the "sons of Israel." In their history they were dispersed from their homeland "for many days... without king or prince." They have abandoned their pagan cult practices and so are "without pillar and teraphim." They have also abandoned the Jerusalem worship, so are "without sacrifice and (literal) ephod." They have lost whatever claim they had to the Aaronic priesthood by the death of their claimant to Aaronic descent in 1623, and so are "without (figurative) ephod." Thus it is not unwarranted to suggest that this remnant of Israel has fulfilled the predictions of Hos 3:4 and is in the initial phase of fulfilling Hos 3:5.

The Jews. The amalgamation of Ephraimites to Judah combines with the possibility that Hosea had the whole Israelite nation in mind, providing our final alternative for studying the fulfilment of Hosea chapter 3, namely in the history of the Jews. As we noted earlier, most scholars recognize that many Ephraimites blended with Judah after the destruction of the Northern Kingdom.[35]

(1) *Political History.* After the Babylonian exile, Judah remained a vassal of Persia. At least for a time, its leadership was derived from the Davidic line, e.g., Zerubbabel. A degree of independence was achieved by the Maccabean revolt of the second century BC, though this was under the leadership of a family of Levitical rather than Davidic descent. This independence was lost when the Romans entered the area in 63 BC. Following the destruction of Jerusalem and the temple in AD 70, most of the Jews were scattered throughout the Roman empire. After the Bar Kochba rebellion was put down in AD 135, the central hill region of

Judea was essentially depopulated of Jews. Despite the devastations, however, a form of Jewish government remained. John Urquhart notes:[36]

Within 60 years after the revolt under Barcochebas the Jews in the Roman Empire ranged themselves under the patriarch of Tiberias, while the Jews in the Persian dominions gave their allegiance to another of their number who bore the title, the Prince of the Captivity [Exilarch, or *Resh Galuta*]. Both sovereignties flourished for a time. The Patriarch [*Nasi*] was permitted to appoint ministers [rabbis], to exercise religious authority, and to receive an annual contribution from the Jews scattered throughout the Empire. "Even now," says Origen, "when the Jews are under the dominion of Rome, and pay the didrachma, how great, by the permission of Caesar, is the power of their Ethnarch! I myself have been a witness that it is little less than that of a king. For they secretly pass judgments according to their law, and some are capitally condemned, not with open and acknowledged authority, but with the connivance of the Emperor." The Prince of the Captivity assumed a still greater state. His installation was marked by great ceremony. The magnates of the people assembled in a magnificent chamber adorned with rich curtains, and the Prince was seated on a lofty throne. He resided in a stately palace, and when he went to pay a visit to the sovereign a royal carriage was placed at his service. But the Patriarchate withered away and was brought to a close about 429. And the last Prince of the Captivity perished on the scaffold at the beginning of the eleventh century. An independent kingdom of the Jews, which had been established in Arabia Felix more than a century before the Christian Era, was overthrown by the Mohammedans in the seventh century.

Ben-Sasson provides us with further details:

The office [of exilarch] was retained by a member of the house of David without any interruption whatever as a result of the transition from Persian rule to Moslem rule....

Until 825 the person recognized by the Jews as their exilarch was also the only Jewish authority acknowledged by Moslem rulers. His status was unquestioned both internally and externally. In that year disputes broke out among the Christians; they too appointed their own heads, who were recognized by the Moslem authorities. As a result of these disputes, the caliph proclaimed that any man accepted by ten infidels as their head would be accorded official recognition. In theory, this pronouncement opened the way to anarchy in leadership and to a complete collapse of the exilarch's authority. In practice, it did lead to a decline in his real power and to a measure of dependency on the two Babylonian *yeshivot* [rabbinical schools] and their heads. However, as a result of the high esteem in which Jewry held the house of David and the desire for one single authority recognized by the host society, during the entire period under consideration here [7th to 11th centuries], apart from relatively few disputes, there was one sole exilarch of the Islamic dispora.[37]

As long as central religious leadership of the Jews remained stable and the political and communications structure of the Moslem caliphate stood firm, the new social forces emerging within the Jewish community... operated within the setting of the established principles. Eventually, however, the caliphate broke up into independent kingdoms, and the ties between the periphery and the centre of the empire were broken.... Leaders in distant countries sometimes received a title from the members of the old centres in Babylonia or Erez Yisrael, whose recognition and approval they still sought. This tie, however, gradually became a matter of tradition, a relic of the past that survived through sheer inertia.[38]

In brief, south of the Pyrenees and west of Erez Yisrael, local communities began to emerge from the end of the eleventh century. It is possible that local leaders had begun to liberate themselves from the central authority even earlier, as a result of the tension between Erez Yisrael and the Babylonian centres. In fact, this tension had on occasion led to the establishment of two separate communities and synagogues... in a single place; and strained relations between them compelled the local inhabitants to conduct their affairs independently.

The rise of a limited territorial leadership certainly contributed to the success of the local community....

In the settlements of Jewish merchants north of the Pyrenees, there was no tradition of submission to any centre at all. The exilarchs, the *geonim* and the *negedim* of the Islamic territories were far away, not only physically but also in terms of the barrier that existed between Christians in north-western Europe and Islam.[39]

Thus by the end of the eleventh century, the Jewish Diaspora was fragmented into local leadership due to the cultural and religious divisions which had developed both within and between Western Christendom and the Islamic East.

This fragmentation was not overcome on any large scale until the latter half of the nineteenth century, when a fresh uprising of Anti-Semitism occurred, reaching its climax in this century's persecutions by Stalin and Hitler. Specific tragedies like the Mortara affair (the kidnapping of a six-year-old from his Jewish parents in Bologna by the Papal guard in 1858) also helped foster a spirit of unity for the sake of self-defense.[40]

Since 1881, and particularly after World War 2, the return of the Jews to their homeland has become significant. The formation of the independent state of Israel in 1948 marks the end of the period when the "sons of Israel" were without "king or prince," as in Old Testament terminology the modern government is at least based on "princes."

(2) *Religious History.* As regards our prophecy, this aspect of Judah's history may be stated briefly. Josiah desecrated the altars and pillars of both Northern and Southern Kingdoms about 624 BC (2 Kings 23). The Babylonian exile itself "did generally succeed in purging" the Judahites from the worship of idols.[41] Thus from post-exilic times the Judahites have been "without pillar and teraphim." It is also apparent that the literal ephod of the high priest was lost or destroyed during the exile, as the Jews no longer had the Urim and Thummim at the time of Ezra (Ezr 2:63).

The loss of sacrifice and priesthood (figurative ephod) occurred with the destruction of the temple in AD 70. Milman suggests that the entire priesthood perished at this time.[42] The *Encyclopaedia Judaica*, on the other hand, believes "the priests merged with the rest of the nation" and also that about 20 years after the destruction, the Sanhedrin at Jabneh [Jamnia] ruled the temple "sacrifices were... replaceable by charity and repentance."[43] In any case, by about AD 100, the Jews are "without sacrifice and (figurative) ephod." This situation has continued to the present day.

Conclusions

We have seen that the prophecy of Hos 3:4 has been fulfilled in the history of the Israelite nation as a whole and therefore in the history of those Ephraimites who amalgamated with the Judahites. It has also been fulfilled in the history of the Samaritan sect. This prophecy did not merely predict a general dispersion of the "sons of Israel," but it detailed *six specific cultural features* of which the Israelites would be deprived. These included native kingship and lesser national rulers, (orthodox) sacrifice as well as idolatrous cult ritual (specifically pillars), the priestly ephod (either the priesthood itself or the specific garment) and idols. The absence of these features has characterized those Jews who have not assimilated into the nations from at least the eleventh century AD. Most of these aspects of the prediction were fulfilled much earlier. The clarity of the prophecy was such as to be recognized by many medieval Jewish scholars; for instance, David Kimchi noted: "These are the days of our present captivity, for we have neither king nor prince of Israel, but are under the rule of the nations, even under the rule of their kings and their princes."[44]

Some may object that the fulfilment of these prophetic details took centuries, that the political decline of the Jews was marked by a long, gradual decline in central authority. This is true, but it is *not uncharacteristic* of a number of Biblical prophecies. While God sometimes chooses to work in dramatic and sudden ways (e.g., the fall of Jerusalem), other prophecies were gradually fulfilled (consider the end of Eli's family's tenure in the high priesthood).[45] The speed of fulfilment is not a criterion in the Bible for estimating the certainty of fulfilment. In fact, long-range predictions fulfilled in recent times manifestly rule out human foresight as an explanation; they serve as valuable evidence for the inspiration of Scripture for our own day.

Within these five verses of Hosea 3 we find a phenomenon difficult to explain on human terms. How could Hosea guess the future state of Israel and get these particular cultural details right? *We need not guess.* Hosea tells us how he obtained his information. The God of the Bible, who controls the historical process and who is willing to forgive those who repent and turn from their sins, told Hosea what the future of His chosen people would be. The God of the Bible (and none other) has demonstrated His power to mold history in order that we might trust in Him and His promises.

What is the next step in Hosea's prophecy? We have already noted that the recent return of many Israelites to their homeland apparently marks the beginning of the fulfilment of verse 5. This verse's reference to "David their king" is almost universally recognized as messianic. Kimchi says, "Wherever it is said, 'in the last of the days,' it means the days of the Messiah."[46] God's period of "many days" is drawing to an end as we near the time of Messiah's return and believers look forward to the millennium and beyond. Perhaps the next step in the fulfilment of Hosea's prophecy is one which we should take ourselves:

Since everything will be destroyed in this way [at Messiah's return], what kind of people ought you to be? You ought to live holy and godly lives as you look forward to the day of God and speed its coming.... So then, dear friends, since you are looking forward to this, make every effort to be found blameless and at peace with him (2 Pet 3:11-12, 14).

But we know that when he appears, we [who believe with all our hearts] shall be like him, for we shall see him as he is. Everyone who has this hope in him purifies himself, just as he is pure (1 John 3:2-3).

Chapter 8

The Return of the Jews

Eugenie Johnston

Ever since 1948, there has been excitement among Bible believers. Biblical prophecy was fulfilled in the establishment of a Jewish state after an interim of nearly nineteen centuries. On top of that, the state of Israel is located in Palestine, just as predicted.

Those who reject the Bible as any sort of revelation from God will naturally feel that this is probably some kind of fundamentalist interpretation *after* the fact, or at best a lucky *coincidence*. In fact, however, something like this was indeed predicted in the Bible. It was recognized by more literal interpreters of prophecy long before it actually came to pass.[1]

The Interpretation of Isaiah 11

The prophet Isaiah, centuries before the time of Jesus, predicted the Jews would return to their land. What exactly did he say? What did he mean? First let us look at Isa 11:10-16 to see what it says. Then we shall look at history to see what has happened.

(10) In that day the Root of Jesse will stand as a banner for the peoples; the nations will rally to him, and his place of rest will be glorious.

(11) In that day the LORD will reach out his hand a second time to reclaim the remnant that is left of his people from Assyria, from Lower Egypt, from Upper Egypt, from Cush, from Elam, from Babylonia, from Hamath, and from the islands of the sea.

(12) He will raise a banner for the nations and gather the exiles of Israel; he will assemble the scattered people of Judah from the four quarters of the earth.

(13) Ephraim's jealousy will vanish, and Judah's enemies will be cut off; Ephraim will not be jealous of Judah, nor Judah hostile toward Ephraim.

(14) They will swoop down on the slopes of Philistia to the west; together they will plunder the people to the east. They will lay hands on Edom and Moab, and the Ammonites will be subject to them.

(15) The LORD will dry up the gulf of the Egyptian sea; with a scorching wind he will sweep his hand over the Euphrates River. He will break it up into seven streams so that men can cross over in sandals.

(16) There will be a highway for the remnant of his people
that is left from Assyria, as there was for Israel when they came
up from Egypt.

Every commentary seems to give a *different* interpretation of this
passage! Much of this variation depends on one's view of the millennial
kingdom of Christ, as this prophecy seems to be closely connected with
that kingdom. All agree that verse 11 speaks of two separate returns of
Israel, but whether the Jewish people would *literally* return to their
homeland or whether they would return to God wherever they live is
disputed. So is the question of whether literal Jews are indicated or
spiritual "Jews," the Christian church. Most writers living before the state
of Israel was founded in 1948 saw no reason to expect the Jews to resettle
as a nation in Palestine.

Commentators also tend to interpret this passage verse-by-verse (in
itself commendable), but in the process they often lose sight of the broad
context, the overall flow of thought in which we must see the interpretation of Isa 11:10-16. As a result, a survey of commentaries is of little
value here. Rather, we must use the basic principles of interpreting the
prophetic sections of Scripture to find out what Isaiah meant. We will
use the following principles, derived inductively from Scripture itself:

1. The purpose of predictive prophecy is *practical*. Mickelsen says:
Prophecy does have a future aspect. But the prediction of
God's doings was given to a particular historical people, to
awaken and stir them. They might not grasp all the meaning of
the message, but the message -- with the disclosure of future
things -- was given to influence the present action.[2]

2. Prophecy is structurally *different* from history writing, whether one
claims it was written before or after the event. In this sense, it is *not*
history written in advance. The history writings of the Bible give a
relatively full account of the events narrated, with time relations clearly
stated. Prophecy gives neither a full account of events nor a clarification
of all time relations. Prophecies are thus somewhat *enigmatic*, never quite
satisfying our curiosity. But after the event, the fulfillment is recog-
nizable.[3]

3. The *time-perspective* of prophecy is often unusual. "Widely
separated events on the actual calendar of history may appear together in
the prophetic sequence."[4] This is understandable because the prophet is
sometimes seeing several events which are all far in the future to him.

4. The message may be set in *culturally dated* terms. We might then
expect these to be fulfilled either (a) literally in all their details; (b)
figuratively or symbolically; or (c) by their equivalents, analogs, or
corresponding cultural terms at the time of fulfillment.[5] For example, the
appearance of swords and horses in a prophecy might indicate alternatively: (a) battle occurring after the collapse of modern technology; (b)
warfare, whatever the technology; (c) equivalent military equipment at the

time of fulfillment, whether rifles and jeeps, or laser guns and hovercraft!

Let us keep these principles in mind as we examine both the flow of thought in Isaiah chapters 1-12 and the details of our particular passage.

Chapters 1 through 12 of Isaiah form a single unit. Two major themes are handled: (1) Israel's two kingdoms, Ephraim and Judah, have rebelled against God; therefore he will punish them by invasion and exile. (2) God will restore Israel as a glorious nation over which the Messiah will be king. Though this latter prediction will apparently be fulfilled in a future far distant to Isaiah, both themes were *relevant* to the prophet's time: the former to call the ungodly to repentance; the latter to give comfort to the godly, who would naturally dread the coming invasion and exile since they believed Isaiah's message.

The outline of Isaiah 1 through 12, below, indicates the interplay of these themes.

Themes in Isaiah 1-12

1:1-31	Introduction to and summary of whole book: Judah's rebellion against God condemned; punishment threatened; God's offer of grace refused
2:1-5	Restored kingdom of Israel under God
2:6-22	Punishment of Judah and of all idolatry
3:1-4:1	Punishment of Judah
4:2-6	God's kingdom restored
5:1-30	Punishment of both Ephraim and Judah; invasion and exile for a rebellious people
6:1-13	Isaiah's vision: invasion and exile
7:1-25	Judah not to be harmed by Syria and Ephraim; invasion of Judah
8:1-22	Syria, Ephraim and Judah to be invaded by Assyria
9:1-7	Messiah's kingdom over Israel
9:8-10:4	Destruction of Ephraim
10:5-34	Punishment of Assyria; a remnant of Jews to return

11:1-12:6   The Messiah's kingdom over restored Israel

Notice that these themes are not presented in a logical order, but rather Isaiah switches back and forth from one to the other somewhat abruptly. His arrangement of material seems to be more emotional, or even symphonic, than coldly logical.[6]

How does this affect our view of chapter 11? After the introduction in chapter one, Isaiah stresses the theme of *judgment*. He touches on restoration only twice, each time briefly, in chapters 2 and 4. Instead, the theme of judgment is built up to a terrible and hopeless climax in chapter 8. Perhaps, however, this was too much for the godly Israelites to bear. The rest of the passage now emphasizes the theme of *restoration and comfort*. Chapter 9 opens briefly on this theme, then returns to judgment, but now of Ephraim only, not Judah. This is the last time punishment for Israel is mentioned; the rest is comfort. Israel's oppressor Assyria will be punished; the Jews will return. Chapters 11 and 12 form the climax of hope, describing in much greater detail the Messiah and his kingdom. Chapter 13 moves on to a different theme -- God's punishment of the nearby nations -- which extends to chapter 21. We therefore treat it as another section.

Looking at chapters 11 and 12 in more detail, our outline looks like this:

The Messiah's Kingdom, Restored Israel

11:1-5   The character and works of the Branch (Messiah)

11:6-9   The resultant conditions of life in his kingdom

11:10-16   The regathering of Israel to their land

12:1-6   The restored Israelites return to God in salvation
            and thanksgiving

This analysis brings 11:10-16 into sharper focus. Before the Messiah can reign over a restored kingdom of Israel, the Israelites must return to their old homeland (11:10-16). Then (chapter 12) they will return to their God.

Let us now look at each verse of Isa 11:10-16 to determine just what is predicted. Here the proper principles of interpreting prophecy and the exact ranges of word meanings are important.

Verse 10. In that day the Root of Jesse will stand as a banner for the peoples; the nations will rally to him, and his place of rest will be glorious.

The "Root of Jesse" is clearly the Messiah, who is to be a descendant of David (and David's father was Jesse). In Isa 11:1ff, he is specifically identified as the ruler of the kingdom. He will be a "banner" for the peoples. The Hebrew word means either "a sign, miracle" or "a high pole, standard, or rallying point."[7] Isaiah goes on to explain how the Messiah will be a banner: the nations will rally to him.

The last phrase, "and his place of rest will be glorious," is puzzling. The Hebrew word *menuhah* means "resting place" or "state or condition of rest."[8] The context does not indicate whether Isaiah meant some physical *location*, such as the restored Jerusalem, or some *state of rest*, perhaps spiritual or physical, after the end-time battles. If the latter, neither does he indicate whether this is the Messiah's own rest or the rest he gives others. All these alternatives would make good sense.

The phrase "in that day" does not necessarily mean these events will occur within twenty-four hours, any more than it does in modern English. It does suggest some temporal connection with the preceding verses.

Verse 11. In that day the LORD *will reach out his hand a second time to reclaim the remnant that is left of his people from Assyria, from Lower Egypt, from Upper Egypt, from Cush, from Elam, from Babylonia, from Hamath, and from the islands of the sea.*

We may or may not have a time gap between verses 10 and 11, depending on how long a "day" is envisioned. Since they are given in this order, it is reasonable to think that the events of 11 follow those of 10, unless the context indicates the contrary.

Isaiah says that the LORD will *twice* reclaim the remnant of his people. The Hebrew is very emphatic about this. The word *qanah*, here translated "reclaim," also means "buy, purchase, own, possess, acquire, get." It may also be used of God as "victoriously redeeming his people."[9] It tells *what* he will do, but does not say *how*.

This verse does not tell us who "the remnant" is, but the following verses clearly point to the Jews. The phrase "that is left" suggests attrition, perhaps by persecution, with only some survivors, in line with our discussion in chapters 6 and 7, above. This interpretation is supported by parallel prophecies but is beyond the scope of this chapter.

The remnant is to be reclaimed from several *specific* lands. Since the prophets presumably wrote in terms their original hearers would understand, we should probably take these names to refer to places at the time of fulfillment described in terms of the names they bore in Isaiah's time. The term "islands of the sea" was apparently used by the Israelites not only to refer to the islands of the Mediterranean Sea, but also to its coastal regions and *anything beyond*.[10] In any case, the reference to "the four quarters of the earth" in verse 12 serves to generalize this specific list to cover most of the world.

Verse 12. He will lift up a banner for the nations and gather the exiles of Israel; he will assemble the scattered people of Judah from the four quarters of the earth.

The first clause may just restate what was said in verse 10 about the Messiah being the banner for the peoples, yet the context is somewhat different. Isaiah predicts that the Jews, who were in Israel when he wrote, would be scattered all over the earth. Even so, God would somehow bring them back. Verse 11 refers to a second regathering. God is to bring the scattered Jews back to Palestine in preparation for the Messiah's reign over restored Israel. This conclusion is implied by the flow of Isaiah 11 and 12.

Verse 13. Ephraim's jealousy will vanish, and Judah's enemies will be cut off; Ephraim will not be jealous of Judah, nor Judah hostile toward Ephraim.

This prediction is made against the background of the divided Israelite kingdoms. Separated by the rebellion of Jeroboam against the house of David in 931 BC, the southern kingdom Judah and the northern kingdom Ephraim were constantly rivals and often at war until the northern kingdom was destroyed by the Assyrians in 722 BC. Early in Isaiah's career, Judah was threatened by Ephraim and Syria (see Isa 7:1-9). Here in our passage, Isaiah predicts that this division will no longer exist in the restored Israelite kingdom. The external enemies will also be destroyed, but not (see verse 14, below, and 11:4) until after some conflict.

Verse 14. They will swoop down on the slopes of Philistia to the west; together they will plunder the people of the east. They will lay hands on Edom and Moab, and the Ammonites will be subject to them.

This verse indicates military conquest of neighboring territories by Israel. The peoples mentioned need not be *physical* descendants of these ancient people (whose descent is probably now impossible to trace). More likely they refer to the modern geographical equivalents, the people living in the regions where these ancient nations dwelt at Isaiah's time. Some details are given. Israel would capture territories formerly held by their neighbors to the east and southwest. Some will come under Israeli domination.

Verse 15. The LORD will dry up the gulf of the Egyptian sea; with a scorching wind he will sweep his hand over the Euphrates River. He will break it up into seven streams so that men can cross over in sandals.

The key problem here is the identity of the "gulf of the Egyptian sea." Is this the northern end of the Red Sea? The Suez Canal? We don't know. It appears that some water barrier is removed to return from Egypt. The reference to "Euphrates" is actually more vague than given here; the Hebrew has "the river," which however normally means the Euphrates. The parallelism of "scorching wind" with "dry up" suggests some supernatural action, rather like that in the opening of the Red Sea at the exodus (Ex 14:21-22), which is explicitly referred to in verse 16.

Verse 16. There will be a highway for the remnant of his people that is left in Assyria, as there was for Israel when they came up from Egypt.

The reference to a "highway" is rather obscure. The comparison with the exodus may indicate a figure of speech, that as the opening of the Red Sea was a "highway" for the Jews to escape Egypt, so now the drying of the Euphrates will be a "highway" for the Jews to escape the territory of Assyria. Whatever the details, it appears that God will somehow facilitate the immigration of Jews from Assyria to Israel.

Having gone through the passage verse-by-verse, let us summarize what it seems to be saying. Taken in the context of Messiah's earthly kingdom, and of a prior regathering of Jews to their ancient homeland, the predictions are as follows: (10) The Messiah is the rallying point of peoples in that they seek him and he provides a glorious rest. (11-12) God will, a second time, reclaim surviving Jews from the lands of their dispersion, including the known world of the time and unknown lands beyond. (13) The nation of regathered Jews will be united, without the envy and warfare which had previously existed between the two divided kingdoms of ancient Israel. (14) Israel will conquer lands to the east and southwest. Some of these people will become subject to Israeli authority. (15-16) God will dry up the gulf of the Egyptian sea and the Euphrates so they will no longer be obstacles to those who wish to cross, thus facilitating the return of the Jews from Egypt and Assyria.

The Fulfillment of Isaiah 11

It is important to be cautious in judging whether or not particular predictions have as yet been fulfilled in history. What may seem at first sight to be the fulfillment may, on careful analysis, prove not to be so. If the fulfillment seems to be occurring in recent years or at present, the need for care is even greater. The current situation can change rapidly and unexpectedly; events in the more distant past have, so to speak, settled down, and their significance may be seen in better perspective. With these points in mind, let us examine possible fulfillments of Isaiah's prophecy.

Verse 10. This prediction could refer to the conversion of people from every nation to the Messiah, Jesus. Such a conversion of Gentiles to the Messiah is predicted elsewhere in Isaiah (42:6; 49:6), and, as we shall attempt to show in coming chapters, Jesus is the promised Messiah. Certainly Jesus is the banner or rallying point for Christians of all nations. The word translated "resting place" or "rest" might then refer to the salvation from sin which he provides, by which he gives rest from condemnation and from self-righteousness to those who trust in him.

If this verse is taken as belonging to the section under discussion (11:10-16), it would point to Christians in the present age, before Jesus' return. If, on the other hand, it is taken with the previous section (11:6ff), it would speak of the rest enjoyed in the Messiah's earthly kingdom after his return. Which of these is intended is unclear. In the former case, the prophecy is being fulfilled throughout church history; in the latter, it is still to be fulfilled.

Verses 11 and 12. If God is to reclaim Israel a second time, it is natural to ask, "What was the first time?" Some have suggested that the deliverance from Egypt under Moses was the first occasion.[11] But Isaiah says God will twice reclaim a *remnant* of Israel, whereas *all* of Israel went out of Egypt with Moses. A better possibility for the first time is the return of a remnant from Babylonian and Assyrian exile after Cyrus authorized the rebuilding of the Jerusalem temple in 537 BC. In verses 11 and 12, Isaiah only alludes to the first return, giving no details by which to identify it. Yet, as mentioned above, one of the major themes of Isaiah chapters 1-12 is the exile of rebellious Israel. Isa 10:20-27 hints at a return of exiles after the fall of the Assyrian empire. Isa 44:26-45:8 explicitly predicts the return under Cyrus. We suggest the return from Babylonian and Assyrian exile was the "first time."

Could it be that the "second time" in Isa 11:11-12 refers only to the return from Babylonian exile? If so, Jews would have had to return from all the areas mentioned by Isaiah: Assyria, Lower Egypt, Upper Egypt, Cush, Elam, Shinar, Hamath, and the islands of the sea. Where did the exiles carried off by Assyria and Babylon *go*, and from whence did they *return* to Palestine?

Between 733 and 701 BC, it is estimated that the northern and southern kingdoms of Israel had a population of between 1.1 and 1.35 million.[12] By 586 BC, most of these were gone; Judea was virtually deserted. The northern kingdom fell to Assyria in 722, and the survivors were deported and resettled in Assyria and Media (2 Kings 17:6). Josephus, writing centuries later, says they were taken to Media and Persia.[13] Nebuchadnezzar conquered Jerusalem in 586, and then completed a series of deportations from the southern kingdom to Babylon begun some years earlier (2 Kings 24:14-16; 25:7; Jer 39:9). Only a few of the poorest Jews were allowed to remain in Palestine, and these soon fled to Egypt (Jer 43:7). So the Jews were exiled to Assyria, Media, Babylonia, Egypt, and possibly Persia.

As far as the return is concerned, Cyrus' decree encouraged Jews, wherever they lived in his empire, to return to Jerusalem (Ezra 1:1-4; 2 Chron 36:23). About 50 thousand Jews from Babylon returned immediately under Zerubbabel (Neh 7:6-7, 66-67). Nearly a century later, Nehemiah led another group from Shushan in Persia (Neh 1:1; 2:1-11). No other places are mentioned from which Jews returned. Among the names of Jews who returned, we find a number of Babylonian and Persian names, indicating that the Jews had lived in these areas,[14] but no evidence of return from other regions.

This return of Jews to Palestine, then, does not fit the prophecy of the second return in Isa 11:11-12 for *two* reasons. (1) The Jews in the

Assyrian and Babylonian exile were not scattered as widely as Isaiah implied they would be, at least until the Greco-Roman period. (2) They were not regathered from all the areas mentioned, but only from Babylon (Shinar) and Persia (Elam). See figure 1 for a map indicating this. Instead the return of Jews to Palestine under Zerubbabel and Nehemiah seems to be the first return implied by Isaiah's use of "second time" in verse 11.

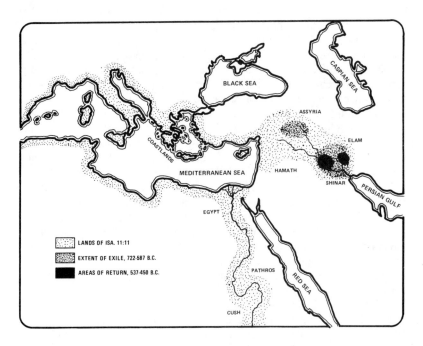

Figure 1. Exile and Return

What, then, is the second return of which Isaiah speaks? To see whether or not this has yet occurred, let us trace the movements of the Jews since the Babylonian exile.

Only a minority of the Jews returned to Jerusalem with Zerubbabel and Nehemiah. Most stayed where they were, and gradually continued to spread throughout the known world. By the time of Esther and Xerxes (486-465 BC), there were Jews in all the provinces of the Persian empire from India to Ethiopia (Est 8:9). The conquests of Alexander (334-323 BC) began their spread westward from Palestine, and by the first century AD, Jews could be found all over the Roman empire (e.g., Acts 2:8-11). Until AD 70, the Jews continued to live in the own land as a national entity, though subject to the dominant empires, whether Persian, Greek or Roman. Finally, however, the Jews rebelled against Rome, and the Romans destroyed Jerusalem and the Jewish state in two wars, AD 66-73 and 132-135. From that time until recently, there has been only a small struggling Jewish population in Palestine and no Jewish state.

Thereafter, the Roman rule over Palestine was marked by warfare along the empire's eastern frontier, which included occasional rebellions by the Jews followed by Roman reprisals. Most of the time, the Palestinian Jews were poor and persecuted, though they received some relief from dispersed Jewish communities outside Palestine.[16]

In AD 379, the Roman empire split east and west; Palestine came under the eastern half, ruled from Constantinople (Byzantium). The *Byzantine* emperors, nominally Christian, established a flourishing economy and church in Palestine, but persecuted the Palestinian Jews so that many either converted or departed.[17]

Between 630 and 640, Palestine was conquered by *Arab Muslims*, and most Jews felt this was an improvement. But in the ninth and tenth centuries the economy failed and confusion developed, in which the Jews suffered along with everyone else.[18] This was followed by the Crusades, a period of constant warfare in Palestine in which the Crusaders at first killed many Jews. Yet the Crusades also opened up trade between Europe and the Middle East, which greatly benefited Palestine.[19]

In 1291, the *Egyptian Mamelukes* drove out the Christians and cut off Palestinian trade. The economy sagged, and with it, the population fell. Constant warfare among petty rulers caused general suffering, which was even worse among the Jews. Yet even so, the greater terrors of the Inquisition and the expulsion of the Jews from Spain in 1492 caused many refugees to flee to Palestine.[20]

Between 1512 and 1516, the *Turks* took Syria and Palestine. They restored order and rebuilt the economy, with the result that the Jews flourished in the sixteenth century. A mixture of good and bad rulers followed, but by 1799, when Napoleon was campaigning in the Middle East, the population had again been reduced to abject poverty.[21] Europe again became interested in Palestine, and conditions gradually improved.

During all these centuries, though a few Jews were always living in Palestine and some came fleeing persecutions in Europe and elsewhere, there was no real regathering of Jews from the lands of their dispersion as Isaiah envisioned. Certainly, no nation of Jews was formed, here or elsewhere, Messianic or not.

But during the mid-nineteenth century, the idea of a Jewish state began to grow in the minds of some pious rabbis in eastern Europe and, independently, in the thoughts of several Englishmen. European Jews began to send financial aid to the relatively backward Jewish communities of the Middle East, though without notable effect. As late as 1882, only 24,000 of the 450,000 inhabitants of Palestine were Jewish.

Suddenly severe persecution broke out in Russia, and hundreds of thousands of Jews fled that land, most to other places in Europe. But among the refugees, a few idealists, joined by others from Rumania and Poland, came to Palestine and founded communities. Although the communities were not very successful, the number of Jews in Palestine rose, and by 1914 it had more than *tripled* to 85,000.

During World War I, the Turks dealt severely with the Jews in Palestine, with the result that their number dwindled to 56,000 by the end of the war. Yet in 1917, in return for Jewish help in World War I, the British government (in the so-called Balfour Declaration) pledged its support to establish a national home in Palestine for the Jewish people.

In 1920, Britain assumed control over Palestine as a mandate from the League of Nations. However, the Arab majority of Palestine had no desire for it to become a Jewish state, and British military administrators there tended to favor Arab interests. As a result, the Balfour Declaration was almost ignored. Even so, there was renewed Jewish immigration to Palestine, and many new communities were established.

During the thirties and early forties, the shadow of Nazi anti-semitism spread over Europe, leading to increased Jewish immigration to Palestine. But this was matched by growing Arab opposition to Jewish settlement. In the midst of increasingly violent Arab-Jewish hostilities were the British, under fire both figuratively and literally from both sides. To keep the peace in Palestine while fighting World War II in Europe, the British sought to stop Jewish immigration in spite of the plight of east European Jews fleeing Hitler's holocaust. The Jews, in their desperation, turned to illegal immigration.

When the war ended, Britain refused to continue its mandate to administer Palestine. The United Nations, which had replaced the defunct League of Nations, partitioned Palestine into an Arab and a Jewish state, in spite of strong Arab objections. When the British withdrew and the partition was put into effect, the surrounding Arab nations immediately invaded the new Jewish state. Almost miraculously, the Jews turned back the Arab armies, and Israel became a free nation in 1948.[22]

The subsequent Arab-Israeli wars of 1956, 1967, 1973, and the Lebanese invasion of 1984-85 are fairly common knowledge. We cannot say for sure what the immediate future of Israel will be, but there is now a Jewish state in Palestine for the first time since AD 135, nearly two thousand years ago. Is this the return that Isaiah predicted? Perhaps the following statistics can help us decide.

Table 1

Jewish Population of
Palestine-Israel, 1856-1967

Year	Population
1856	10,500
1882	24,000
1895	47,000
1914	85,000
1922	83,800
1931	174,600
1939	449,500
1948	758,700
1951	1,404,400
1961	1,981,700
1967	2,383,600

Source: *Encyclopaedia Judaica*, 5:1502

Table 1 shows there has been an enormous growth in the Jewish population of Palestine in the past century, increasing by a factor of more than 200 in the period indicated. This is astronomically larger than the growth rate of the world Jewish population, indicating a *substantial shift* of population to Israel. As table 2 shows, less than one-half of one percent of the world Jewish population was in Israel at the turn of the century, but now almost twenty percent is there. Clearly, there has been a dramatic return of Jews to Palestine in this century, though the majority are still in dispersion.

What have been the *sources* of Jewish immigration to Palestine, and how do they relate to the countries mentioned in Isa 11:11? The population trends for Jews in these specific countries are sketched below.

The ancient countries of Lower Egypt (*Mizraim*), Upper Egypt (*Pathros*) and Cush are included in the modern nations of Egypt and Sudan, perhaps also Ethiopia. In 1947, Egypt's Jewish population was 66,000. By 1967, it had dropped dramatically to 2500.[23] In fact, by 1970, only four Jewish families still lived in Egypt; 35,000 Jews of Egyptian origin lived in Israel, and 47,000 in France, Great Britain, the United States and Argentina.[24] The Jews of Egypt had seen both prosperity and persecution. But since the founding of Israel in 1948, anti-Jewish sentiment has been strong, with riots and confiscation of property leading many Jews to leave.[25] The resurgence of Islam in the Sudan and of Marxism and famine in Ethiopia is doubtless encouraging Jewish departure from these lands, though we do not have figures for this.

Table 2

Proportion of Jews in Israel

Year	Jews in Israel	Jews in World	Proportion
1895-1900	47,000	10,602,000	1:225
1939	449,500	16,724,000	1:38
1948	758,700	11,373,000	1:15
1967	2,383,600	13,837,500	1:6

Source: *Encyclopaedia Judaica*, 5:1502; 13:891-2, 895

Assyria and Babylon are largely the modern country of Iraq. The Jewish population of Iraq has likewise declined drastically, from 150,000 in 1947 to 2500 in 1967.[26] Between 1948 and 1950, in reaction to official harassment and confiscation at home, about 123,000 Iraqi Jews settled in Israel.[27]

Hamath was a city on the northern border of ancient Israel when the country was its largest in the times of Solomon. Hamath and part of ancient Assyria are now in modern Syria. Persecution of Jews under the influence of Arab nationalism has been especially strong in Syria since 1947, and has resulted in a drop in the Jewish population from 15,000 to 3000 as of 1968. This emigration was particularly substantial in view of efforts by the Syrian government to discourage it by freezing the bank accounts and confiscating the property of departing Jews.[28]

Ancient Elam, later called Persia, is Iran today. As of 1968, fewer Iranian Jews had migrated to Israel than from other Middle Eastern countries. In 1948, Iranian Jews numbered 95,000. By 1968, this had fallen to 60,000, with 55,276 Jews migrating to Israel from Iran between 1950 and 1968.[29] This was doubtless due to a more favorable climate for Jews in the Shah's regime. Since the Shah was overthrown by radical Shi'ite Muslims under Ayatollah Koumeini, the migration has increased. As of the end of 1983, there were only about 27,000 Jews still in Iran.[30]

From the foregoing information, graphically summarized in figure 2, it appears that most of the Jews living in the specific nations mentioned in Isa 11:11 have left these countries, and most of these have gone to Israel. The immediate cause of the migration is primarily persecution, but the prophecy does not say how God would regather Israel. Jews from all over the world ("the four quarters of the earth," verse 12) have also moved to Israel, although large numbers still remain in the more industrialized nations.[31]

Figure 2

Jewish Population in Middle Eastern Countries

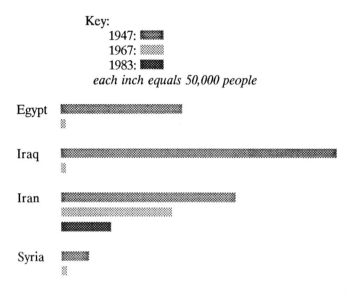

Key:
    1947: ▨
    1967: ▨
    1983: ▨
each inch equals 50,000 people

Egypt

Iraq

Iran

Syria

Source: mostly *Encyclopaedia Judaica*

Verses 13-16. Continuing with our verse-by-verse examination of fulfillment, these verses suggest some of the events in Israel in recent decades. There is no longer a political division of the Jews into two separate nations as there was in Isaiah's time. Though there are certainly conflicting political parties in Israel, the same was true in each of the two nations in antiquity. Thus verse 13 has clearly been fulfilled in the new Jewish state of Israel.

Verse 14 might well describe the military campaigns of Israel since 1948. The "slopes of Philistia" would be the low hills in the southwest, possibly extending to the Gaza strip. These were taken in the 1948 and 1967 wars, respectively. The ancient nations of Ammon, Moab and Edom all fall within present-day Jordan and the Negev. Some of this territory was taken in 1948, and Jordan lost all its West Bank territories in 1967. Yet the situation in the Middle East continues to be very unstable, and we are still too close to the events described to be sure of such interpretations.

Verses 15 and 16 are rather enigmatic. Possibly the reference to the drying up of the "gulf of the Egyptian sea" relates to the cutting off of the

Suez Canal, as happened in 1973. More likely the verses predict miraculous events. Presumably they are as yet unfulfilled.

Conclusions

From this study, it appears that Isa 11:10-16 is in the *process* of fulfillment. Jesus the Messiah has been and is the rallying point of those from many nations who have trusted him as Savior. He has given them rest by a glorious means -- through his incarnation, death and resurrection.

In our own century, God has begun to reclaim a second time a remnant of Jews who are left, from the nations surrounding Palestine in particular, but also from all over the earth. He has assembled them in Palestine, and by a series of marvelous providences, has formed a new Jewish nation, the first such to exist in almost 2000 years. This new nation is no longer divided as Ephraim and Judah were in Isaiah's time. So far, they have managed to dominate their neighbors militarily in a way that was impossible when the prophet wrote.

The history of Israel is *not over yet*, and if the Bible is right, the Jews will face troubles in the future that will make Hitler's holocaust pale.[32] Yet there is clearly a match between the main features of Isa 11:10-16 and Israel's recent history, a fit of such a striking nature that one should consider seriously the claims of the Bible to be God's word. If the God of the Bible really exists, it is most important that we pay attention to what he says about our own eternal destiny.

Part Three

Prophecies about
the Messiah

Chapter 9

The Person
of the Messiah

Robert C. Newman

Various people and events are predicted by the Old Testament prophets. None is more intriguing than the promised deliverer who is to come and rescue Israel from its enemies. This person is known both to Jews and Christians as the Messiah.

In the centuries around the beginning of the Christian era, many Jews tried to piece together the scattered Old Testament references to the Messiah in order to figure out who he was, what he would do, when he would come, and such. The situation at that time was rather like that in evangelical Christianity today, where there are lively discussions concerning the time and nature of the events relating to Christ's second coming as pictured in the New Testament.

Fortunately a number of records have survived from antiquity which preserve information about Messianic speculation at that time. The earliest such material is found in the so-called *apocalyptic literature* -- the Book of Enoch, the Testaments of the Twelve Patriarchs, the Sibylline Oracles, 2 Baruch, and 4 Ezra, to name but a few -- dating from the second century BC to the second century AD.[1] The discovery of the Dead Sea scrolls, a whole library belonging to a Jewish monastic community at Qumran, has added to such material, providing early manuscripts of apocalyptic literature and also discussions and Biblical commentaries from about the time of Jesus.[2]

Also from the first century AD we have writings by early *Christians* preserved in the New Testament. According to these records, the Old Testament prophecies of the Messiah were applied to one Jesus of Nazareth by Jesus himself and his immediate followers. In the first few centuries following the time of Jesus, the oral traditions and debates of the rabbis concerning Messianic prophecy were written down in the *rabbinic literature*. The most extensive collection of this literature is the *Babylonian Talmud*.[3]

During these centuries the Old Testament prophecies about the Messiah functioned as the available "data" (if we may borrow some terminology from science), from which were constructed various "models" or "theories," each of which attempted to produce a unified picture of the coming Messiah or Messiahs. Several "apocalyptic models" were produced, including a "Qumran model"; there was a "New Testament model" or "Christian model"; and there were several "rabbinic models" for the Messiah. In this chapter, we shall compare these models with one another and, most important, with the *Old Testament data*. We shall see that the New Testament model turns out to be clearly superior to its competitors in fitting the OT data.

In science, whenever two or more models have been proposed to explain some phenomena, researchers try to design a crucial experiment to distinguish between the models, one which will rule out all but one model, or at least demonstrate its clear superiority. In our case, as in any historical investigation, experiments are not possible. Yet we may still seek certain *crucial data* which perform a similar function. In fact, the Old Testament data concerning the Messiah contains several *paradoxes* which make it especially difficult to construct a satisfactory model. A model which is able to handle these paradoxes will be clearly superior to those which cannot.

This particular form of argument is important today, since liberal theologians seek to rule out any appeal to fulfilled prophecy as evidence for Christianity. Liberals often charge evangelical Christians with bias, claiming that they "ransack the Old Testament" to find passages which may be twisted into predictions of Jesus. Evangelicals, on the other hand, feel the liberal rejection of the miraculous begs the whole question of the truth of Biblical Christianity, which is nothing if it is not miraculous. Any investigation which can carry us back to the time of the coming of Jesus will allow us to experience, to some extent, the impact these prophecies had on the ancients. It will allow us to see another reason why Christianity experienced such astonishing growth at the very time Judaism ceased to be a missionary religion.

We will not prejudice this investigation by examining passages which only the New Testament claims to be Messianic, nor by rejecting passages which modern liberalism has doubted are Messianic. Instead we shall consider only passages which were thought to be Messianic by the ancient *rabbis*.[4]

The Office of the Messiah

The word *Messiah* is borrowed by English directly from the Hebrew word meaning "anointed one." Similarly *Christ* is borrowed from the Greek word with the same meaning. The words refer to the practice of ceremonially pouring perfumed olive oil on the head of a person to designate him as God's choice for some important task. In the Old Testament, both the high priest and the king of Israel were anointed when they assumed office. Thus the question naturally arises, "Is the predicted Messiah to be a king or a priest?"

Apparently, the Jewish sect at Qumran expected *two* Messiahs. Their *Manual of Discipline* speaks of the coming of the "Messiahs of Aaron and Israel."[5] Since the high priest is a descendant of Aaron and the king ruled over all Israel, most scholars think this refers to a king-messiah and a priest-messiah.[6]   This idea was probably not unique to Qumran, since the Testaments of the Twelve Patriarchs picture a Messiah from Levi (Aaron's ancestor)[7] and a Messiah from Judah (David's ancestor).[8]

This two-messiah model may seem strange to us, but it is really very reasonable. The Old Testament regulations for Israel kept the priesthood and civil authority strictly separate. Neither Moses, Joshua nor the judges were priests (only Samuel, in a crisis period of Israel's history, comes close). Nor was the kingship given to the descendants of Levi. In fact, when King Uzziah tried to act as priest by burning incense (2 Chron 26:16-21), God struck him with leprosy, stopping his priestly pretensions and effectively ending his kingship as well. Thus the idea that a coming king and coming priest should be separate individuals would be rather deeply ingrained in Jewish thought.

From this perspective it is rather surprising that the New Testament sees the Messiah as a *single* person who is *both* king and priest. For instance, Heb 1:8 clearly pictures Jesus as king, while chapters 3 through 10 of the same letter discuss his priestly activity. Seen in the light of the general Old Testament background, this would seem to cut across a carefully laid distinction, almost as though the author of Hebrews was a Gentile unfamiliar with the Old Testament Scripture.

In fact, however, this is one of the *paradoxes* of the Messianic prophecy of the Old Testament. Though the Old Testament regulations carefully keep the two offices separate, this is probably intended to make the Messiah stand out as the one who *combines* the two in one person. Psalm 110, recognized as Messianic in pre-Christian times,[9] speaks of God establishing someone as ruler (vv 1-3) who is also priest (v 4): "The LORD has sworn and will not change His mind: 'You are a priest forever in the order of Melchizedek.' " But just because of the strict separation of kingship and priesthood in Israel, it was necessary for the writer of Psalm 110 to go all the way back to Genesis, centuries before Israel became a nation, to find in the mysterious figure of *Melchizedek* (Genesis 14) an example of a righteous person who is both priest and king!

Here, then, we see that the Qumran model of two Messiahs, though initially most reasonable, has failed to deal with a significant Messianic passage. Because it seems to go against the general tenor of the Old Testament, Psalm 110 was apparently ignored, without considering why God might have kept such a strict separation. In the important question of the office of the Messiah, the New Testament model is clearly superior, solving a significant paradox.

The Work of the Messiah

As the Messiah is a king, we naturally expect part of his work to be *ruling*. In this we are not disappointed, as a large number of Old

Testament passages speak of the reign of the Messiah.[10]

We also saw from Psalm 110 that the Messiah is a priest. However, there are few passages which speak explicitly of his priestly activity. Besides Ps 110, there is only the rather difficult revelation given in Zech 6:12-15. The prophet Zechariah, apparently acting out a parable at God's instruction, makes a gold and silver crown from the contributions of Jewish exiles. He places it on the head of Joshua the high priest. Speaking of someone called "the Branch," Zechariah says:

> Here is the man whose name is the Branch, and he will branch out from his place and build the temple of the LORD. It is he who will build the temple of the LORD, and he will be clothed with majesty and will sit and rule on his throne. And he will be a priest on his throne. And there will be harmony between the two. (Zech 6:12-13)

That Joshua is intended to be the Branch seems unlikely, since Zechariah then removes the crown and places it in the temple as a memorial. This is confirmed by Zech 3:8, where the prophet says: "Listen, O high priest Joshua and your associates seated before you, who are men symbolic of things to come: I am going to bring my servant, the Branch."

Though there are few passages which picture Messiah acting as priest, there are a number of prophecies which describe some figure who is to *suffer*, and whose suffering is to produce unusual results. Psalm 22, for instance, pictures one who suffers unto death but then is delivered. The story of what has happened is to be spread throughout the world and down to future generations. Isaiah 53 speaks of a despised sufferer who bears the sins of others to his grave. Afterwards he is delivered and so exalted that kings are amazed. Zech 12:10-13:9 pictures one who is pierced. As a result, Israel will mourn and then be cleansed from sin. These passages were all understood to refer to the Messiah in ancient rabbinic literature.[11] Indeed, in one early rabbinic view, the Messiah is called " 'the leper scholar,' as it is written, 'Surely he hath borne our grief, and carried our sorrows: yet we did esteem him a leper, smitten of God and afflicted.' " (Isa 53:4)[12]

By the second century AD, however, the rabbinic model has come to include two Messiahs. These are not a king and priest as at Qumran, but a king and a *general*. The general is called "Messiah ben Joseph" or "Messiah ben Ephraim." He is to appear at the end of the age prior to the king Messiah, called "Messiah ben David." He will lead the return of Israel to Palestine, set up a government and temple worship, but then suffer and die in battle against the Gentile enemies of Israel.[13] The suffering passages of Old Testament Messianic prophecy are assigned to *him* rather than to the king Messiah. In contrast to this rabbinic model, the New Testament applies both the suffering and ruling predictions to *one* person, Jesus of Nazareth. Isaiah 53 is associated with him about forty times and Psalm 22 about twenty-five times. Zech 12:10 is applied to Jesus twice, in John 19:37 and Rev 1:7.

Who is right? It is noteworthy that Zech 12:10, "*They* shall look on me whom *they* have pierced," is explicitly assigned to Messiah ben Joseph by the rabbis.[14] But unless one arbitrarily applies the first "they" to Israel and the second to the Gentiles (for which there is no support in the context), it looks like the "pierced one" has been injured by Israel! This does not fit the rabbinic picture of Messiah ben Joseph (killed by invading Gentiles), but it certainly fits the New Testament model.

Similarly, Isa 53:10, in which God makes the sufferer's "life a guilt offering," fits the New Testament model nicely; the letter to the Hebrews presents Jesus as sacrifice as well as priest. But this whole sacrificial aspect, a central feature of New Testament Christianity, is *missing* in the Messiah ben Joseph and in the rabbinic outlook in general.

The Coming of the Messiah

Let us next consider the *coming* of the Messiah, not *when* he is to come (the subject of the next chapter) but *how* he is to come. Although the questions, "Is he to come as a child or as an adult?" and "Is he to come publicly or secretly?" are of considerable interest, let us further limit our discussion to another aspect, namely, "Is the Messiah's coming to be one of *exaltation or lowliness*?"

Naturally, since the Messiah is a king sent from God, one would expect his coming to be *glorious*. This is the picture we get from Dan 7:13-14:

> In my vision at night I looked, and there before me was one like a son of man, coming with the *clouds of heaven*. He approached the Ancient of Days and was led into his presence. He was given authority, glory and sovereign power; all peoples, nations and men of every language worshiped him. His dominion is an everlasting dominion that will not pass away, and his kingdom is one that will never be destroyed.

Thus the one receiving a universal, everlasting kingdom is to come "with the clouds of heaven," something like the so-called *Shekinah* glory of Mt. Sinai, the wilderness wanderings and the temple.[15]

On the other hand, Zech 9:9 presents a lowly coming:

> Rejoice greatly, O daughter of Zion; / Shout, O daughter of Jerusalem: / Behold thy King cometh unto thee; / He is just and having salvation; / Lowly and riding on an ass / And upon a colt the foal of an ass.

Following the rabbinic model mentioned above, one would like to assign *this* verse, with its lowly coming, to Messiah ben Joseph, but Dan 7:13-14, above, to Messiah ben David. However, Messiah ben Joseph is *not* a king (since kingship was given to David's descendants, of the tribe of Judah), yet the rider in Zech 9:9 is explicitly called a king. This verse thus presents a serious problem to the rabbinic model.

Two attempts have been made to blunt the force of this difficulty. One is to see Zech 9:9 as actually an *exalted* coming. When the Persian emperor Shapur jokingly offered to lend the Jews a horse so their Messiah would not have to come on a donkey, Rabbi Samuel retorted, "Do you have a hundred-colored horse?"[16] Samuel thus implies that the Messiah's mount will be no ordinary animal, but something supernatural. This suggestion, however, suffers from the problem that Zech 9:9 explicitly calls the king's coming "lowly."

The other attempt was proposed by Rabbi Joshua.[17] He suggested that Daniel 7 and Zechariah 9 picture *alternative possibilities* rather than both actually occurring. If Israel is worthy, the Messiah will come "with the clouds of heaven." If not, he will come "lowly and riding upon an ass."

The New Testament, on the other hand, pictures these two comings as *real and successive*: the Messiah comes first in lowliness, to suffer and die for his people's sins; later, he returns in power to rescue his people, judge his enemies and reign forever. This certainly gives a better fit with the Old Testament data, as there is no indication in the contexts that Daniel 7 and Zechariah 9 are merely alternative possibilities. In fact, the New Testament is able to *connect* the lowly coming with Messiah's sufferings (as the rabbis cannot) just because the suffering Messiah is the *same person* as the coming king. He may therefore be designated "king" by the prophet (Zech 9:9) even at his lowly coming. Here again, we see the superiority of the New Testament model in handling the paradoxes of the Old Testament data.

The Nature of the Messiah

Having examined the office, work and coming of the Messiah, let us consider his nature. What *sort of being* was the Messiah to be?

As the Messiah is frequently called the son of David, it would be most natural to assume the Messiah is *purely human*. This seems to have been the view of some of the apocalyptic writers[18] and of later rabbinic Judaism, where the humanity of the Messiah, perhaps in reaction to Christianity, came to be emphasized to the neglect of any superhuman features. Thus when Rabbi Akiba (2nd cen AD) proposed that one of the thrones in Dan 7:9 should be for God and another for David (a name for the Messiah), he was sharply rebuked by Rabbi Jose the Galilean: "Akiba, how long wilt thou treat the Divine Presence as profane! Rather, it must mean, one for justice and one for grace."[19] Not even the Messiah was to be placed in such close proximity to God!

Other apocalyptic writers, however, saw the Messiah as more than merely human. For instance, the Assumption of Moses says of the coming Messianic king:

And then His kingdom shall appear through His whole creation. And then the devil shall have an end, and sadness shall be taken away with him. Then the hands of the Angel shall be filled, who is established in the highest, who shall avenge them of their adversaries. For the Heavenly One shall arise from the throne of His kingdom, and shall come out of His holy habitation.[20]

Here the Messiah seems to be called "the Angel." Similarly, in the book of Enoch, in a passage alluding to Daniel 7:

And then I saw One who had a head of days, and His head was white like wool, and with Him was another being whose countenance had the appearance of a man, and his face was full of graciousness, like one of the holy angels.[21]

Thus some of the apocalyptic writers saw the Messiah as *angelic* or as a *combination* of man and angel.

The New Testament pictures the Messiah as a man, of course, but also as *much more than a man*. With its doctrine of the virgin birth, the New Testament transcends even the apocalyptic models of an angelic Messiah. The New Testament model appears to be unique in picturing the Messiah as *divine*.

But in fact the New Testament is *not* unique at this point. The Old Testament data includes passages which require the New Testament model! For instance, Micah 5:2 says:

But as for you, Bethlehem Ephrathah, Too little to be among the clans of Judah, From you One will go forth for Me to be ruler in Israel. His goings forth are from long ago, From the days of eternity.

Although this passage does not *require* the deity of the Messiah, it does necessitate his *pre-existence*. This person will have been active for a very long time (the Hebrew is consistent with either a finite or infinite period), yet he will claim a Judean village, Bethlehem, as his hometown. Apparently the Messiah will be born and yet have existed long before his birth. Some of the rabbis, to avoid this conclusion, picture the Messiah, after having been born in Bethlehem, as waiting incognito for *centuries* until Israel should be worthy of his coming, meanwhile doing good deeds by bandaging lepers at the gates of Rome![22]

That the Messiah should be *both* son of David and pre-existent is occasionally seen in the apocalyptic literature,[23] probably because of Old Testament passages like this. But because no one knew how to reconcile the two ideas, they were not emphasized as they are in the New Testament.

Another such passage is Isa 9:6:

For to us a child is born, to us a son is given, and the government will be on his shoulders. And he will be called Wonderful Counselor, Mighty God, Everlasting Father, Prince of Peace.

The next verse makes it clear that this person is the Messiah, for he is to rule forever from the throne of David.

That this person will be born is even clearer here than in Micah 5:2, yet so is his deity. Though strenuous attempts have been made to weaken the titles given this person,[24] the conjunction of title, his eternal rule and his pre-existence perfectly fit a being who is both God and man.

This New Testament model, which joins both deity and humanity in one person, also explains some other puzzling problems: (1) how the sufferer of Isaiah 53 can bear the sins of many; (2) how the king of Ps 45:6 can be addressed as God; (3) how the priest-king of Psalm 110 is called "Lord" by his father David; and (4) why the death and revival of the sufferer in Psalm 22 and Isaiah 53 is so important both to Israel and the Gentiles. These are mysteries in the other Messianic models.

Conclusions

In this chapter, we have seen the superiority of the *New Testament* model of the Messiah to its competitors in fitting certain paradoxical Old Testament references concerning the office, work, coming and nature of the Messiah. This not only indicates that the God of the Old Testament is the One who controls history and announces "the end from the beginning," but also that the New Testament and its Messiah are the continuation and fulfillment of his revelation to mankind.

This line of argumentation is also important because it presses us to make a choice without waiting "until all the data is in." We should not be surprised that this is so, for we are forced to do this in making most of our decisions in everyday life. No scientific theory, in fact, is ever based on an induction from *all* the data. We are confronted right now with the Bible's answers to life's crucial questions, with God's demands on us, and with our unwillingness and inability to obey him satisfactorily.

There is yet another point of superiority for the New Testament model of the Messiah. Unlike the other models, it also presents an actual historical figure as candidate for its Messiah, *Jesus of Nazareth*. Most historians will concede that this Jesus has had as great an impact on history as any man who has ever lived. Yet this New Testament model is put forward as Jesus' own explanation of his person and work, not just the assessment of later centuries.

Finally, the New Testament, written in the lifetime of people who personally observed Jesus' ministry, reports that he rose from the dead; that he demonstrated himself to be alive to hundreds of men and women who later died rather than renounce their testimony; that he ascended to heaven to await his second coming.

May *we* not wait for his return before we turn back to him in repentance and trust, so that his suffering two thousand years ago may prevent our suffering for all eternity.

Chapter 10

The Time
of the Messiah

Robert C. Newman

According to ancient historians, the first century AD was a time of unusual expectation among the Jews. The feeling was widespread that some prophecy regarding the time of Messiah's coming was about to expire. The Roman historian Suetonius (early 2nd cen) says of the Jewish revolt against Rome (AD 66-73):

> There had spread over all the Orient an old and established belief, that it was fated at that time for men coming from Judaea to rule the world. This prediction, referring to the Emperor of Rome, as afterwards appeared from the event, the people of Judaea took to themselves.[1]

Suetonius' contemporary Tacitus also speaks of this prophecy, supplying more information about its source:

> ... in most there was a firm persuasion, that in the ancient records of their priests was contained a prediction of how at this very time the East was to grow powerful, and rulers, coming from Judaea, were to acquire universal empire. These mysterious prophecies had pointed to Vespasian and Titus, but the common people, with the usual blindness of ambition, had interpreted these mighty destinies of themselves, and could not be brought even by disasters to believe the truth.[2]

Closer to the scene, and writing less than ten years after the fall of Jerusalem in AD 70, was the Jewish historian Flavius Josephus. Josephus wrote before Titus succeeded his father Vespasian as emperor, and he indicates only a single expected ruler:

> But now, what did most elevate them in undertaking this war was an ambiguous oracle that was also found in their sacred writings, how "about that time, one from their country should become governor of the habitable earth." The Jews took this prediction to belong to themselves in particular; and many of the wise men were thereby deceived in their determination. Now this oracle certainly denoted the government of Vespasian, who was appointed emperor in Judea.[3]

Josephus' application of the prophecy to his patron Vespasian is understandable, but it is doubtful that his fellow Jews agreed! In any case, a large number of them were ready to follow Bar-Kochba in another disastrous revolt only sixty years later, when Rabbi Akiba proclaimed him Messiah.[4]

By the middle of the third century, however, a mood of resignation had set in among the Jews. The scholar Rab admitted that "all the predestined dates have passed." He explained the apparent delay of the Messiah by suggesting that his coming now awaits Israel's repentance and good works.[5]

So ancient sources, both Jewish and pagan, indicate that Old Testament prophecy foretold a time for the coming of the Messiah, which time expired in the first century AD. What prophetic passage or passages did they have in mind? These sources do not tell us, but from early times Christians have believed that Dan 9:24-27 gives us just such a prediction:[6]

(24) Seventy "sevens" are decreed for your people and your holy city to finish transgression, to put an end to sin, to atone for wickedness, to bring in everlasting righteousness, to seal up vision and prophecy and to anoint the most holy.

(25) Know and understand this: From the issuing of the decree to restore and rebuild Jerusalem until the Anointed One, the ruler, comes, there will be seven "sevens" and sixty-two "sevens." It will be rebuilt with streets and a trench, but in times of trouble.

(26) After the sixty-two "sevens," the Anointed One will be cut off and will have nothing. The people of the ruler who will come will destroy the city and the sanctuary. The end will come like a flood: War will continue until the end, and desolations have been decreed.

(27) He will confirm a covenant with many for one "seven." In the middle of the "seven" he will put an end to sacrifice and offering. And on a wing [of the temple] he will set up an abomination that causes desolation, until the end that is decreed is poured out on him.

Sir Robert Anderson's Calculation

There is considerable disagreement among Christians as to how the details of this passage were fulfilled in the coming of Jesus.[7] Currently the most popular interpretation of this passage is that given by Sir Robert Anderson.[8] He pinpoints the end of the sixty-ninth "seven," the coming of Messiah, as Sunday, April 6, AD 32, claiming this was the very day of Jesus' triumphal entry into Jerusalem.[9]

In brief, Anderson identifies the command "to restore and rebuild Jerusalem" (Dan 9:25) with the permission given Nehemiah by the Persian king Artaxerxes I (Neh 2:6) to rebuild the city. Neh 2:1 tells us this occurred in the month Nisan of the king's 20th regnal year. Assuming that this command was given on the first day of the month, Anderson locates the starting point at March 15, 445 BC.

Since the Messiah is to be cut off after the first sixty-nine "sevens" (7 + 62), we should be able to calculate when this would occur. Virtually all commentators, liberal or conservative, agree that the "sevens" (often translated "weeks") of the prediction are periods of seven *years*. If so, 483 years (69 x 7) after March 15, 445 BC carries us to March 15, AD 39, some years after Jesus' public ministry ended.

Therefore, Anderson assumes that a special kind of year is being used in the prophecy, which he calls a "prophetic year," consisting of only 360 days, rather than our solar years of just under 365 and 1/4 days.[10] This assumption is based on Rev 11:23, where Anderson equates a period of 42 months with a period of 1260 days. These would be exactly equal if each month were 30 days long, and twelve such months would have 360 days. With this adjustment, Anderson converts from solar years to prophetic years and finds the 69th week ending at April 6, AD 32.

Unfortunately, Anderson's view faces some serious problems. First of all, Anderson arbitrarily chose the first day of the month Nisan as his starting point[11] even though the Bible gives only the month, not the day. But if Anderson started even a week later, his 69th week would end after the crucifixion.

Second, Anderson's equation of the first of Nisan with March 15, 445 BC, is based on modern astronomical calculations. But it is not possible from such information to locate the beginning of these ancient months so exactly. The first day of the month depends not only on the location of sun, moon and stars in antiquity (which modern astronomers can calculate), but also on the (weather-dependent) observations of these bodies by the ancients from which they made their decisions regarding when to begin a new year or month. For this we need *historical* as well as astronomical information. There is thus some question about the location of Anderson's starting point.

Third, Anderson has used a 360-day "prophetic year" to measure the length of the period. But the Old Testament connects the Passover festival, in the middle of Nisan, with the offering of first-ripe grain (Lev 23:6-14), so that the Jewish calendar must remain *synchronized* with the seasons. Both archaeology and the rabbinic literature indicate that this synchronism was accomplished by adding an extra lunar month every two or three years to the 354-day lunar "year,"[12] so that in the long run the average length of the Jewish year just matches our solar year of about 365 and 1/4 days.

Nor does Rev 11:2-3 require a 360-day "prophetic year." This passage does not say that the Gentiles will tread the holy city under foot for forty-two months *to the day*. Using our modern months and years (virtually the same as used by Rome when Revelation was written), a 1260-day period is about 41 and 1/2 months, which might easily be rounded off to 42. Using the Hebrew lunar months averaging 29 and 1/2 days each, 1260 days are just over 42 and 1/2 months. Thus the 42 months and the 1260 days may be approximately rather than exactly equal. There is no reason to believe the Bible defines some sort of "prophetic years" of special length.

There is also some question whether Jesus' crucifixion occurred in the year AD 32. Suggestions range from AD 29-33, with the consensus at present favoring AD 30.[13] Even given the exact year, locating the date of Passover (and "Palm Sunday" before it) involves the same problem of combining modern astronomical calculations and ancient calendar decisions mentioned above. There are thus serious problems identifying April 6, AD 32 with Jesus' triumphal entry into Jerusalem.

Yet in spite of these objections, a good case can be made for a real fulfillment of this prophecy, even though the result is not quite so spectacular as Anderson's. In addition, this alternative suggestion, which we give here,[14] arises much more naturally from the context of the passage.

The Context of the Seventy Weeks Prophecy

To understand this prophecy of the seventy "weeks," let us look at its context. The prophecy itself, Dan 9:24-27, was given the prophet in answer to his prayer recorded in Dan 9:4-19. The occasion of the prayer is found in verses one and two of the same chapter. Daniel has just understood from "books" that the desolation of Jerusalem would last only seventy years. The time has apparently nearly elapsed, so he prays that God's promise may now be fulfilled.

What are these "books"? Jeremiah's prophecy is obviously one of them, since Jeremiah is mentioned by name. But what other book or books might have been involved? The second book of Chronicles also mentions the seventy years' captivity (36:21), but as it goes on to describe Cyrus' decree allowing the Jews to return to Palestine, it had not yet been written when Daniel made his prayer. However, the writer of Chronicles does explain that the length of the captivity was seventy years to compensate for seventy *sabbath-years* in which the Jews had disobeyed God's command to let the land lie fallow.

The command instituting the sabbatical year is found in Ex 23:10-11 and Lev 25:3-7, 18-22. The Exodus passage reads: "For six years you are to sow your fields and harvest your crops, but during the seventh year let the land lie unplowed and unused."

In addition to these passages establishing the sabbatical year, Lev 26:32-35 predicts that exile would come upon Israel if they violated the sabbath-year regulation:

> I will lay waste the land, so that your enemies who live there
> will be appalled. I will scatter you among the nations and will
> draw out my sword and pursue you. Your land will be laid waste,

and your cities will lie in ruins. Then the land will enjoy its sabbaths all the time that it lies desolate and you are in the country of your enemies; then the land will rest and enjoy its sabbaths. All the time that it lies desolate, the land will have the rest it did not have during the sabbaths you lived in it.

Perhaps, then, Exodus and Leviticus are the other books Daniel consulted. At least these provided all the materials necessary to reach the conclusions given in 2 Chronicles -- that the length of Israel's exile would correspond to seventy sabbath years they had neglected. Perhaps Daniel had been thinking about this God-ordained land-use cycle and the period of seventy such cycles during which Israel had disobeyed this ordinance. If so, the message which the angel brought him, "Seventy weeks have been decreed for your people..." seems less obscure. Apparently Dan 9:24-27 uses the term "seven" (or "week") for the Old Testament sabbath year cycle.[15]

Interpretation of Daniel 9:25-26

In our discussion, we shall consider in detail only the *coming* of the Messiah, that is, just the first sixty-nine weeks of Daniel's seventy. As far as the seventieth week is concerned, some see this as fulfilled immediately after the 69. Yet the passage itself seems to suggest a gap of indefinite length between the 69th and 70th weeks. Thus the destruction of the (temple) sanctuary mentioned in verse 26 is followed by a summary statement of war and desolation to the end. Then verse 27 speaks of a covenant which apparently introduces the 70th week, followed by an interruption of sacrifices, which seems to presuppose a rebuilt temple. In this view, the 70th week is still future and belongs to the class of yet-to-be fulfilled prophecies. In any case, this is beyond our concern here.

To calculate the time of the coming of the Messiah, we must consider the 25th and part of the 26th verses of Daniel chapter nine. The translations of the *New American Standard Bible* and the *New International Version* are similar,[16] indicating one Messiah who comes at the end of 7 + 62 weeks. Having given the NIV above, we cite the NASB here:

> So you are to know and discern that from the issuing of a decree to restore and rebuild Jerusalem until Messiah the Prince there will be seven weeks and sixty-two weeks; it will be built again, with plaza and moat, even in times of distress. Then after the sixty-two weeks the Messiah will be cut off and have nothing...

On the other hand, the *Revised Standard Version* is characteristic of a group of translations[17] which have two "Messiahs" or "anointed ones," one coming after 7 weeks and another cut off after an additional 62 weeks:

Know therefore and understand that from the going forth of the word to restore and build Jerusalem to the coming of an anointed one, a prince, there shall be seven weeks. Then for sixty-two weeks, it shall be built again with squares and moat, but in a troubled time. And after the sixty-two weeks, an anointed one shall be cut off, and shall have nothing...

The translation of the RSV group follows the Masoretic punctuation of the Hebrew Bible, where a division in the sense is made between seven weeks and sixty-two weeks.[18] But such punctuation may not date back before the ninth or tenth century AD.[19] This rendition does, however, explain the occurrence of the peculiar combination 7 and 62 instead of their sum 69.

In spite of these facts, the parallelism of the passage favors the former alternative. In the Hebrew, the phrase rendered "restore and rebuild" consists of the same pair of verbs as are translated "built again" later in the same verse. Likewise the word "Messiah" is repeated. This parallelism may be sketched as follows:

From the going forth of the word to *build again* Jerusalem

To *Messiah* the Prince shall be 7 weeks and 62 weeks

Plaza and moat shall be *built again*...

And after the 62 weeks *Messiah* shall be cut off.

This parallelism suggests the passage is structured as a *summary* statement of two lines mentioning two events and two time periods, followed by two more lines which give *details* of each event in turn. Thus we would have one Messiah or anointed one, whose coming occurs after 69 weeks from the starting point. Perhaps the first seven weeks, if one may hazard a guess,[20] involve the actual rebuilding of the city.

The Starting Point

Various suggestions have been advanced for the proper starting point of the seventy weeks: (1) God's word at the fall of Jerusalem (586 BC; Jer 25:11-12; 29:10); (2) Cyrus' word in allowing the captives to return to Jerusalem (537 BC; 2 Chron 36:23; Ezra 1:2); (3) Artaxerxes' commission to Ezra (458 BC; Ezra 4:11-12, 23); (4) Artaxerxes' commission to Nehemiah (445 BC; Neh 2:1-6).[21] Of these four, only the *last* actually issued in the rebuilding of the city wall. In thus making Jerusalem fortified, it became, in ancient parlance, once more a *city* and no longer merely a village.

We shall follow this fourth alternative, the same as that used by Anderson. Neh 2:1 dates this to the twentieth year of Artaxerxes I, namely 445 BC. Chronological studies since Anderson's time have not changed the year, though the date of the first of Nisan may be questioned.[22]

The Sabbatical Year

Now we must make the calculation forward from 445 BC. Unlike Anderson, however, we shall use the actual sabbatical cycles as *units* of measurement (rather than just adding 7 x 69 years to the starting point), since this fits better with the context.

Our first concern is to locate these cycles in antiquity if possible, as this will have some influence on the location of the endpoint. The best-known evidence for the location of sabbatical cycles in the period under consideration comes from the first book of Maccabees, a primary historical source for the Maccabean era. There we find that Jewish resistance to the Syrians was on one occasion weakened because their food supplies were low due to the observance of a sabbatical year (1 Macc 6:49, 53-54). A reference earlier in the chapter (6:20) indicates this occurred in the 150th year of the Seleucid era. According to Finegan,[23] the 150th year would be either 163/2 or 162/1 BC, depending on whether the Macedonian or Babylonian calendar was in use.

The *first* of these alternatives fits the modern Jewish sabbatical cycle very well;[24] the year 164/3 would have been a sabbath, so that famine conditions would have been most acute in the following year before crops could be harvested. This modern sabbatical cycle is apparently based on the work of Zuckermann in 1856.[25]

Recently, however, Ben Zion Wacholder has reviewed all the data on which the location of the sabbath cycle was determined, plus additional information not available when Zuckermann made his study.[26] As a result, he finds the modern cycle in error by one year, and he chooses the second alternative allowed by 1 Maccabees. Consequently, 163/2 BC is the relevant sabbath year.[27]

We shall follow Wacholder's suggestion for the sabbatical cycles in making our calculation. It is possible that his cycle may be off by one year.

The Calculation

Using Wacholder's list of sabbatical years,[28] our calculation is very simple. Our starting point, the month Nisan in 445 BC, falls in the seven-year cycle 449-442 BC, of which the last year, from September 443 to September 442, is the seventh or sabbatical year.[29] Using the usual Jewish inclusive method of counting, 449-442 is the *first* "week" of Daniel's prophecy. The second is 442-435 BC, and so on, down to the transition from BC to AD, where we need to remember that 1 BC is immediately followed by AD 1, with no year zero in between (see figure 3).

Figure 3

	445		BC				AD		Jesus	
449		442		435	428		14	21	28	35
	v								+	
1st		2nd		3rd	...		67th	68th	69th	

Thus the 69th cycle following Artaxerxes' giving Nehemiah permission to rebuild Jerusalem is AD 28-35. Just the time that Jesus of Nazareth was "cut off" in Palestine while claiming to be God's Messiah! Some may be concerned that Daniel says "*after* the sixty-two weeks Messiah will be cut off," whereas by our calculation the crucifixion occurs *on* the 62nd week (the 69th, adding the first seven). But this, too, is a conventional Jewish idiom in which "after" means "after the beginning of." Recall that Jesus' resurrection is alternatively spoken of as occurring "*after* three days" (Matt 27:63; Mark 8:31) and also "*on* the third day" (Matt 20:19; Mark 9:31). Even if we follow Zuckermann's scheme for the location of the sabbatical cycle instead of Wacholder's, the 69th cycle only shifts by one year, to AD 27-34, which still fits equally well. Likewise an error by a year or two on either end, for Artaxerxes 20th year or the date of the crucifixion, would not change the result. The prediction fits Jesus even allowing for the largest possible uncertainties in chronology.

Conclusions

There is real force in this prophecy of the seventy weeks. The use of sabbatical cycles is favored by the context. Inclusive counting is the regular Jewish practice. The location of the sabbatical cycles and beginning and end points could be in error by a year or two without changing the result.

The result itself is quite significant for the history of human thought. In pointing out Jesus of Nazareth at a distance of centuries, it deals a powerful blow against the belief that there is no real prediction in history (various forms of theological liberalism), and it condemns the rejection of Jesus as Messiah (Judaism and other non-Christian religions).

Of all the Messianic claimants that Judaism has ever had, the only one considered an outstanding historical and ethical teacher (even by many atheists) *just happened* to conduct his short public ministry and was "cut off" within the period AD 28-35!

Chapter 11

The Work
of the Messiah

Frederick A. Aston

One of the most amazing and beautiful predictions concerning the Messiah is the poem found in the fifty-third chapter of Isaiah, considered by many to be the greatest passage in the Old Testament. As the climax of the so-called Servant section of Isaiah (chs 41-56),[1] it provides a portrait of God's Servant as one who suffers. His work of suffering becomes the solution to the greatest problem facing mankind.[2]

(52:13) See, my servant will act wisely;
      he will be raised and lifted up and highly exalted.

(14) Just as there were many who were appalled at him --
      his appearance was so disfigured beyond that of any man
      and his form marred beyond human likeness --

(15) So he will sprinkle many nations,
      and kings will shut their mouths because of him.
  For what they were not told, they will see,
      and what they have not heard, they will understand.

(53:1) Who has believed our message
      and to whom has the arm of the LORD been revealed?

(2) He grew up before him like a tender shoot,
      and like a root out of dry ground.
  He had no beauty or majesty to attract us to him,
      nothing in his appearance that we should desire him.

(3) He was despised and rejected by men,
      man of sorrows and familiar with suffering.
  Like one from whom men hide their faces
      he was despised and we esteemed him not.

(4) Surely he took up our infirmities
      and carried our sorrows,
  Yet we considered him stricken by God,
      smitten by him and afflicted.

(5) But he was pierced for our transgressions,
      he was crushed for our iniquities;
  The punishment that brought us peace was upon him,
      and by his wounds we are healed.

(6) We all, like sheep, have gone astray,
      each of us has turned to his own way;

And the LORD has laid on him
the iniquity of us all.

(7)   He was oppressed and afflicted,
            yet he did not open his mouth;
        He was led like a lamb to the slaughter,
            and as a sheep before her shearers is silent,
            so he did not open his mouth.
(8)   By oppression and judgment he was taken away,
            and who can speak of his descendants?
        For he was cut off from the land of the living;
            for the transgressions of my people he was stricken.
(9)   He was assigned a grave with wicked men,
            yet he was with a rich man in his death,
        Since he had done no violence,
            nor was any deceit in his mouth.

(10)   Yet it was the LORD's will to crush him and cause him to
            suffer,
            and though the LORD makes his life a guilt offering,
        He will see his offspring and prolong his days,
            and the will of the LORD will prosper in his hand.
(11)   After the suffering of his soul,
            he will see the light [of life] and be satisfied;
        By his knowledge my righteous servant will justify many,
            and he will bear their iniquities.
(12)   Therefore I will give him a portion among the great,
            and he will divide the spoils with the strong,
        Because he poured out his life unto death,
            and was numbered with the transgressors.
        For he bore the sin of many,
            and made intercession for the transgressors.

Who is this Suffering Servant? Three main theories have been
proposed: (1) he represents the people of Israel; (2) he is an unknown
individual; (3) he is Jesus. Before we examine each of these alternatives,
let us analyze the *poem itself* to discover its portrait of the Servant. The
following features characterize the Servant of Isaiah 53.[3] (1) He is
portrayed in detailed features as a real person. (2) He is an innocent
sufferer (vv 4, 5, 8d, 9cd, 12). (3) He is a voluntary sufferer (vv 4, 7ab).
(4) He is an obedient, humble and silent sufferer (v 7). (5) His suffering
springs from love for sinners, including his executioners, who act in
ignorance (vv 4, 12). (6) His suffering is ordained by God in love, and
fulfills the divine intention and purpose (v 10). (7) His suffering is
vicarious or substitutionary (vv 4ab, 5, 6cd, 8d, 10b, 11d, 12e). (8) His

suffering is redemptive and spiritual in nature (vv 5cd, 11c). (9) His suffering ends in death (vv 8ac, 9ab, 10ab, 12c). (10) His death gives way to resurrection (vv 10, 11, 12; 52:13). (11) His atoning work leads the straying people to confession and repentance (vv 4-6). (12) His redemptive work inaugurates a victorious life of kingly glory (vv 10cd, 11ab, 12ab; 52:13, 15).

The Corporate Theory

Can these characteristics really fit the *nation Israel*, either (a) the whole nation *historically*, or (b) a *spiritual remnant* thereof, or (c) the nation *ideally*, as it now exists in the mind of God and someday will really be? Let us examine each point noted in our analysis, above, as they relate to these alternatives.

(1) Could Israel have been *personified* in poetic language which lacks any hint that it is an allegory? There is no parallel case in the Bible where personification is maintained throughout a whole passage without any such indication; rather, distinct hints are always provided in any allegorical passage. Even so liberal a scholar as Bernhard Duhm says:

The Servant of Yahweh is here treated even more individualistically than in the other [Servant] songs, and the interpretation of his person as referring to the actual, or the "true," Israel is here altogether absurd.[4]

(2) Has Israel as a nation been an *innocent* sufferer? The words in v 8, "for the transgression of my people he was stricken," make the application to Israel as the Servant untenable. "My people" clearly indicates Israel. If the Servant is Israel, how can he be stricken for Israel's sins and still be innocent? In our passage the Servant is clearly suffering for others (vv 4-5) and the sacrificial lamb picture is prominent as well (vv 7, 10b). But Israel is not innocent; elsewhere the prophet speaks of Israel as a "sinful nation, a people loaded with guilt, a brood of evildoers, children given to corruption" (Isa 1:4), while in chapter 42 he indicates that Israel's affliction is God's judgment for the nation's *own* sins. The synagogue liturgy for the high holy days contains the following confession: "Because of our sins we have been exiled from our land."

(3) Has Israel been a *voluntary* sufferer? The Jews have never gone voluntarily into captivity. Each exile was the result of a humiliating national defeat.

(4) Has Israel been an obedient, humble and *silent* sufferer? George Adam Smith has well observed:

Now silence under suffering is a strange thing in the Old Testament -- a thing absolutely new. No other Old Testament personage could stay dumb under pain, but immediately broke into one of two voices -- a voice of guilt or a voice of doubt. In the Old Testament the sufferer is always either confessing his guilt to God, or, when he feels no guilt, challenging God in argument.[5]

No sooner was Israel delivered from slavery in Egypt than the people rebelled against every hardship in the wilderness (Ex 17:3; Num 11:1; Deut 1:27). Even such righteous individuals as Job, Moses, David, Elijah and Jeremiah succumbed to the temptation to complain bitterly against their circumstances. The taking of Jerusalem in AD 70 by the Romans was one of the most stubbornly contested sieges in all history. Numerous times the Jewish people have revolted against their oppressors, whether Persian, Syrian, Roman, Muslim or Christian.

(5) Has Israel suffered *in love*? Since Israel's suffering was neither voluntary nor silent, it couldn't very well be "suffering love."

(6) Has the suffering of Israel been *divinely ordained* in love? Of course. All events of history are divinely ordained, and all of God's actions toward his people manifest love. But this is not the sense of verse 10, where God makes the Servant suffer as a guilt offering.

(7) Has Israel suffered *for other nations*? Not according to the Old Testament or early rabbinic literature. Yet the idea of substitutionary suffering and atonement is very prominent in our chapter, being expressed no less than twenty-three times in nine of the twelve verses.

(8) Have the sufferings of Israel *brought redemption* to the world? No, the sin of man is too great and God is too holy for any man to redeem himself, let alone others. The Bible nowhere teaches that Israel will be redeemed by its own suffering, much less that it will redeem other nations, particularly from the power of sin. Nor does it indicate that a few righteous individuals will redeem either Israel or other nations. Recall Ezk 14:12-23, which says that even if Noah, Job and Daniel were in a wicked country, they could only save themselves from its destruction. Israel's sufferings have not only failed to *justify* her oppressors, they have led God to *bring vengeance* on the oppressors; Nazi Germany is an example. Since Israel's sufferings have never been *voluntary*, it is hard to see how they can have such redemptive power.

(9) Have the sufferings of Israel *ended in death*? Certainly for many individuals. Israel as a state died in 587 BC and in AD 70. But whether the historic or ideal Israel be considered, the answer is *no*. Some have seen the exile as a figurative death, but this is not likely. The exile actually served as a purifying force, strengthening the Jewish zeal for God and for monotheism. In fact, the Jewish people are a striking exception to the usual course of a nation's growth and decline. Nearly every other nation that shared the stage with Israel in Old Testament history has long since passed into oblivion. The survival of the Jews is unique. In spite of exile, dispersion, persecution, and attempts to force assimilation, they survive. In spite of liberation and toleration -- often more disintegrating than persecution -- Israel still maintains its racial identity.

(10) Has Israel experienced a *resurrection*? As a state in Palestine, yes. As neither the ideal nor the historic Israel died, there could be no resurrection for them.

(11) Has Israel's suffering produced a *moral transformation* in the nations and caused them to break down in a confession of guilt? No. Throughout the ages, the nations which oppressed Israel were never known to show the attitude expressed in this chapter, where a prominent place is given to confession and repentance.

(12) Has the humiliation of Israel resulted in *glorification*? No. Even if death were taken as a figure for the Babylonian exile, the restoration that followed did not lift Israel to such exaltation as our passage pictures. For Israel to fit into the prophetic picture of preeminence, three things must be true: (a) Israel must have made a voluntary atonement -- one accepted by God as well as by men -- bringing redemption to the world. (b) As a result of this atonement, Israel must have attained a position of great power and glory in the world. (c) Israel must have made intercession for the transgressors. Not one of these three is true of Israel, either the historical, the spiritual or the ideal.

This *first theory*, that the Servant is a *personification* of the Jewish nation, not only fails to fit the twelve features noted above, but it also meets with further serious objections. It forces the following interpretations on the text: verses 1-10 have the Gentile nations speaking; the death of the Servant symbolizes the exile, the end of Jewish national existence; the resurrection is a figure of the restoration of Israel, to be followed by the conversion of the heathen. The insurmountable objection to these interpretations lies in the need for assuming the Gentile nations are speaking in vv 1-10. No Jewish prophet would have represented the heathen as expressing such sublime thoughts and exhibiting the attitude described here. As Gressmann notes: "A penitential psalm in the mouth of the heathen is altogether improbable; the literature of the Old Testament lacks analogous examples."[6]

The view that the Servant means not the whole nation, but just the *spiritual element* within it, also meets additional obstacles. It may be said that the spiritual Israelites suffered most in the exile, and also that they sought to bring the nation to repentance and to spread knowledge of God among the Gentiles. Probably they also met with some persecution at the hands of other Jews during the exile. Yet it is hard to believe that during the exile there was such a *great difference* between the nation as a whole and the spiritual remnant as to account for the language of our passage. While the remnant doubtless recognized that the national calamity was due to the sin of the people, there is no reason to think the remnant was the special object of divine wrath. The pious did not suffer *for*, but only *with*, the nation. The Servant gave his life as a sacrifice, but the remnant, spiritual Israel, did not die in the captivity.

Finally, the view that the Servant personifies *ideal Israel*, existing at present only in the mind of God and becoming a reality only in the future, is also untenable. In our passage, the actual nation is depicted realistically, with all its faults and its greatest sin -- rejecting the Servant, its Redeemer. Do lowly origin, mean appearance, and general repulsiveness characterize the ideal Israel? Can the ideal Israel suffer and die for the actual nation and then rise again?

But is not *Israel* called the Servant in some of the other Servant passages? Yes, this is true (Isa 41:8-9; 44:1-2; 45:4; 48:20; 49:3). Yet the personality of the Servant in Isa 52:13-53:12 *differs* not merely in degree but in kind from the Servant Israel, towering over every other individual in the Old Testament. Here, too, suffering has a new meaning, necessity, purpose and value.

Israel's relationship to God was interrupted when the nation became unfaithful (Isa 42:18-20). The term "Servant of the LORD," originally applied to the nation Israel, then transcends its former limitations and becomes associated with the person and work of the Messiah, who was entrusted with the mission which Israel had so ignominiously failed. As a result, the application of the phrase "Servant of the LORD" to Israel is untenable in a number of passages besides our own (Isa 42:1-7; 49:1-9; 50:4-9), as in these the Servant is *distinct* from Israel, having a mission to fulfill in gathering Israel and in being a light to the Gentiles.

It is a striking fact that the synagogue readings from the prophets always *omit* Isa 52:13-53:12, while the portions immediately preceding and following are read. If the leaders of modern Judaism really believe that this chapter depicts Israel, why don't they read it in public? At a memorial service for the Jews who died in the gas chambers of Auschwitz or in defending the Warsaw ghetto, what could be more comforting than the divine promise: "my righteous servant will justify many, and he will bear their iniquities"? To thousands who mourn relatives lost in the Nazi holocaust, how consoling would be the assurance that their loved ones' deaths were part of God's redemptive plan!

The Individual Theory

We now turn to consider the theory that the Servant of Isa 52:13-53:12 was an *unknown individual*. Some have seen the Servant as a *leper*, translating v 4: "we did esteem him a leper, smitten of God and afflicted." But no leper could have made the offering for sin so clearly described in the passage. Even the animals sacrificed in the temple had to be unblemished. How can the words, "by oppression and judgment he was taken away" (v 8a), implying judicial procedure, and "though he had done no violence, nor was any deceit in his mouth" (v 9cd), indicating a miscarriage of justice, be applied especially to a leper? Likewise being "cut off from the land of the living" (v 8c) is a Hebrew idiom for violent death, not for leprosy. Where in history is there any record of such a leper?

Others see the individual as a *martyr*, perhaps Isaiah or Jeremiah. But such glorification of a pious man, even a martyr, is foreign to the Old Testament. One will search in vain for such a eulogy even of the greatest of Israel's heroes, whether Abraham, Joseph, Moses, or David. Likewise we have no biblical support for the idea that the death of a righteous man would result in the redemption of the Gentile world.

Consequently, strong voices have been raised in support of the view that the Servant is the *Messiah*. Rabbinic literature, including prayers of the synagogue, indicate that ancient Judaism realized that Isaiah was speaking of a person of transcendent influence, who ranks morally and spiritually above any other character in the Old Testament. Thus the passage was applied to the Messiah.

Wuensche has made a laborious compilation of extracts from old rabbinical writings. From these we can conclude that the idea of a suffering Messiah was by no means foreign to ancient Judaism.[7] Emil Schuerer makes a similar inference:

> It is indisputable that in the second century after Christ, at least in certain circles in Jewry, there was familiarity with the idea of a Messiah who was to suffer, even suffer vicariously, for human sin. The portrayal of Justin makes it sure that Jewish scholars, through disputations with Christians, saw themselves forced to this concession. Thus an idea was applied to the Messiah which was familiar to rabbinic Judaism, that is, that the righteous man not only observes all the laws, but through suffering also atones for sins that may have been committed, and that the surplus suffering of the righteous benefits others.[8]

The *Targum Jonathan*, a paraphrase of the prophets recognized as authoritative by the Jews no later than the fourth century AD, opens our passage with "Behold, my servant, the Messiah, prospers."[9] It shows striking inconsistencies, perhaps due to misunderstanding by the interpreter or to later emendations. It applies the glorious parts of the passage to the Messiah and the sufferings to Israel, but it leaves no doubt that some Jews applied Isaiah 53 to the Messiah.

In *Midrash Cohen*, Elijah thus comforts the Messiah:

> Bear the suffering and punishment of Thy Lord with which He chastises Thee for the sins of Israel, as it is written, "He for our rebellions was pierced through, crushed for our iniquities" (Isa 53:5), until the end comes.[10]

The *Midrash Rabbah* of Rabbi Mosheh Haddarshan states:

> Immediately the Holy One, blessed be He, began to put before the Messiah these stipulations, "Messiah, my righteous one, the sins of those hidden with Thee will bring Thee under a heavy yoke: Thine eyes will not see light; Thine ears will hear

great reproach from the nations of the world; Thy nostrils will smell stench; Thy mouth will taste bitterness; Thy tongue will cleave to Thy palate; Thy skin will shrivel upon Thy bone, and Thy soul will be weakened by grief and groaning. If Thou art willing to take it upon Thyself, well and good, but if not, I shall drive them [the generations] out of existence even now." He answered, "Lord of the Universe, I joyfully take upon myself these sufferings...." Immediately the Messiah took upon Himself "the sufferings of love," as it is said, "Torments He endured submissively" (Isa 53:7).[11]

Another Midrash states that in the Messianic age the patriarchs will say to the Messiah:

Ephraim, Messiah Our Righteousness, although we are Thy forefathers, Thou art greater than we, because Thou has borne our iniquities and the iniquities of our children, and there have passed over Thee hardships such as have not passed upon men of earlier or of later time, and Thou wast an object of derision and contumely to the heathen for Israel's sake.[12]

The *Musaph* service for the Day of Atonement contains a remarkable ancient prayer:[13]

Messiah Our Righteousness has departed from us. We shudder; for there is none to justify us. He bears our load of transgression and the burden of our guilt and is verily pierced for our rebellions. He carries our guilt on His shoulder, to effect forgiveness of our sins. He bled for our salvation. O Eternal One, the time has come that Thou shouldest create Him anew! O, bring Him up from the terrestrial sphere. Raise Him up from the land of Seir, to assemble us on Mount Lebanon,[14] a second time, by the power of Yinnon![15]

In spite of the voices raised in ancient Judaism, the illustrious rabbi Rashi (c1040-1105) and the great grammarian David Kimchi (1160-1235) interpreted Isaiah 53 as referring to Israel. Rashi's view became authoritative, perhaps because the massacres of Jews taking place during the Crusades seemed to fit the picture of Israel as the Suffering Servant. Yet so great a scholar as Maimonides (1135-1204) rejected this view as unsatisfactory, not being in harmony with the synagogue liturgy.

As late as the seventeenth century, leading rabbis still applied the chapter to the Messiah. Rabbi Naphtali ben Asher Altschuler (c 1600) says: "I am surprised that Rashi and David Kimchi have not, with the Targum, also applied them [Isa 52:13-53:12] to the Messiah."[16] His contemporary, Rabbi Mosheh Alsheh, says:

I may remark, then, that our rabbis with one voice accept and affirm the opinion that the prophet is speaking of the King-Messiah, and we ourselves shall also adhere to the same view.[17]

Jesus as the Servant

The portrait of the Servant bears striking similarity to that of Jesus of Nazareth, as described for us in the New Testament. In terms of the features noted in Isa 52:13-53:12, we note the following.

(1) He was a historic person (Matt 2:1; Luke 3:1-2). (2) He was an innocent sufferer (John 8:34). (3) He was a voluntary sufferer (John 10:17-18; Gal 2:20). (4) He was an obedient, humble, and silent sufferer (Matt 27:12,14; Phil 2:8; 1 Pet 2:23). (5) His suffering was grounded in love, the redeeming and reconciling love of God (John 3:16), in which his atoning work was accomplished. He loved even his oppressors, who acted in ignorance (Luke 23:34; Acts 3:17). (6) His suffering was the result of a divine plan and fulfilled God's will (Acts 2:23; Eph 3:11). (7) His suffering was substitutionary (John 1:29; 1 Pet 2:24). (8) His suffering was redemptive, a revelation of God's power intervening in history, leading to justification of evildoers by forgiving their sins (Matt 9:12-13; Rom 5:6-9; 1 Pet 1:18-19). (9) His suffering ended in death (Matt 27:50). (10) His death gave way to resurrection (Acts 1:3; 1 Cor 15:3-8). (11) The redemptive purpose of God, realized in the life, death and resurrection of Jesus, will be brought to completion at his second coming, when Israel's national confession and repentance will take place (Zech 12:10; Matt 24:30-31; Rom 11:25-26; Rev 1:7). (12) He ascended to heaven and is now highly exalted, sitting at God's right hand (Luke 24:51; John 6:62; Acts 1:9-11; Phil 2:9-11).

Objections to the identification of Jesus of Nazareth as the atoning Messiah rest either on disbelief in the *predictive abilities* of the Old Testament prophets; or on rejection of Messiah's *twofold nature*, both human and divine, which are not mutually exclusive; or on disregard of his *twofold ministry*: (1) to come as a child in humility to suffer and die for man's sin; (2) to rise from the grave and ascend to take his exalted place at God's right hand, one day to return in glory and triumph.

Yet Isaiah predicted:

My servant will act wisely, he will be raised and lifted up and highly exalted... I will give him a portion with the great... because he poured out his life unto death, and was numbered with the transgressors. For he bore the sin of many, and made intercession for the transgressors.

Chapter 12

Conclusions

In the previous chapters we have looked with some care at a number of predictions made in the Bible. We have seen how these prophecies were fulfilled in remarkable detail, often at a distance of several centuries after the prediction was made. Let us summarize what we have found.

Summary of Prophecies

We first considered various prophecies concerning the nations around Israel. We saw (ch 3) how Ezekiel predicted that Tyre, that great Phoenician trading city, would be destroyed by the combined efforts of many nations, that its debris would be scraped up and thrown into the water, and how this was exactly fulfilled in the campaign of Alexander the Great some 250 years after Ezekiel's time. We also saw (ch 4) how Alexander's campaign on the eastern shore of the Mediterranean fulfilled detailed predictions which Zechariah made some 200 years earlier. Among the Phoenician cities, Tyre was destroyed, but Sidon was spared. As for the Philistine cities, Ashkelon, Ashdod and Gaza were destroyed, but Ekron was assimilated into Judah. Whereas most of the nations in that area were conquered and many peoples were displaced, the Jews were greatly honored and respected. Some centuries earlier (ch 5) Nahum predicted the destruction of Nineveh, capital of the Assyrian empire, about forty years in advance. Nahum rightly noted that Nineveh would be taken by siege, in the summer, after its outlying defenses had been picked off one by one, the city being taken with the help of a flood. Most noteworthy was Nahum's prediction that Nineveh would never rise again.

Next we looked at predictions concerning the Jews. We saw (ch 6) that the disasters threatened to come on Israel in the book of Deuteronomy have been fulfilled in a remarkable way by the tragic history of this people and by no other people on earth. It was predicted that the Israelites would turn from their God to worship idols. As a result they would be oppressed, besieged, enslaved, killed and finally driven from their own land and scattered among the nations. Their exile would be prolonged and harsh, marked by continual oppression and terror. Yet in all this, they would not cease to exist as a people. And just so it has proved to be. We saw (ch 7) how Hosea's succinct statement has characterized Israel for nearly the whole of the past two thousand years: they were to be without king or prince, without Sinai religion or idolatry. Has any other writer ever characterized a nation's history in advance so accurately for such a long period? Finally (ch 8) we noted how the return of the Jews to Palestine in this century has resulted in their regathering from the very places predicted by Isaiah, producing a single united Jewish nation, which has dominated its neighbors militarily just as the prophet said.

Lastly, we considered prophecies concerning the promised Messiah. We noted (ch 9) how certain Old Testament prophecies regarding the office, labors, coming and nature of the Messiah were paradoxical, so that ancient interpreters were unable to devise models which fit the data, but how the New Testament model and its candidate Jesus of Nazareth fit nicely. In addition (ch 10) we noted how Daniel's prophecy of the seventy weeks predicted that the Messiah would be cut off at the very time Jesus was crucified in Jerusalem. Finally (ch 11), we noted how the suffering servant predicted by Isaiah -- a real person who is to suffer voluntarily, obediently, humbly and silently; who is to offer his life in love as an innocent sacrificial substitute for the sins of others; who is to live again after his death, and lead his straying people to confession and repentance -- exactly matches Jesus as pictured in the New Testament.

Implications

What are we to make of all this? Are these merely lucky guesses? No, if we dismiss these evidences as luck, we will have no one but ourselves to blame when we stand before God in judgment. The probability that the Bible writers could have accidentally gotten all these predictions right is astronomically small. Most of us are sufficiently cautious not to cross a busy street as though there were no traffic if we think there is even one chance in a thousand of getting hit by a car. What excuse, then, can we give for crossing life as if there is no God when the evidence from fulfilled prophecy warns us that there is much less than one chance in a thousand we can *avoid* getting hit by the judgment?

Perhaps all the prophecies here were carefully selected by the editor of this book, and the rest of the Bible is really filled with prophecies that never came true. This is not the case. I have, in fact, picked a number of the clearer and more striking prophecies, but there are still many such not discussed here.[1] Of course, there are prophecies regarding the end of the age, the second coming of Jesus, and the last judgment which have not been fulfilled as yet. But I know of no biblical prophecies which have been *disfulfilled*, that is, which have not been fulfilled so far and cannot be fulfilled in the future because some time limit or non-repeatable condition has passed. But you don't have to take my word for it. There is no way we can be sure of such facts without reading the Bible for ourselves. This may be a big job, since it takes nearly a year to read through the Bible at four chapters per day. But it is worth it. We dare not depend on someone else's opinion in so important a matter as this. But please make sure, when you read it, that you do not let the question of whether you *like* what it says divert you from the question whether or not it is *true*. Wishful thinking is a temptation to all of us, and it can have tragic results, especially when we are deciding what life is all about.

Fulfilled prophecy allows us to obtain *objective* answers to the most important questions in life, questions that many have thought unanswerable or, at best, purely subjective. Is there a God? Yes, this universe was created and its history is controlled by the God of the Bible. Does life have meaning? Yes, all life has meaning. The meaning of our lives will be *tragic* if we continue to ignore or rebel against God, but it can be *wonderful* beyond our best dreams if we will acknowledge him and let him take charge of our remaining years.

How can I come back to God? This was answered beautifully in chapter 11, where we saw Isaiah's picture of God's sacrificial lamb, God's perfect substitute. Jesus of Nazareth is totally unique among mankind. As God he is uncreated. As man he is created. No other being in the universe chose to become created; the rest of us were already in existence as created beings before we ever had anything to say about the matter. Therefore no other being could offer his creaturely obedience to God as something he did not already owe. Thus if we trust in Jesus, his righteousness, his perfect obedience to God's law, is credited to our account. Jesus also died a terrible death in payment for sin. Because he was innocent, he did not deserve it himself. Because he is God, he was able to suffer in a few hours what would take us forever. If we trust in him, the punishment we deserve is counted as having been suffered by him.

Thus in Jesus alone the righteousness we lack is provided and the punishment we deserve is paid. And there is more. When we trust in him, God puts within us his own spirit, and we begin to see our whole life transformed. We begin to hate the evil we once loved; we begin to love the good we once hated. We begin to become more and more like Jesus. Though we will struggle, stumble and fall, we will find strength to get up again and press on. We come to see that life is worth living after all; that though we are weak and sinful still, we can now begin to accomplish things that will be worthwhile forever.

Would you like to have a life like that? You can! It can start right now. Just bow your head and talk to God. He can hear you wherever you are. Tell him you're sorry for what you've done and what you've been. Tell him you want to come back to him and be his kind of person. Tell him you know you're not good enough to deserve this, but you're depending on Jesus as your substitute. Ask him to take you back, for Jesus' sake; to change you inside and to make your life count for something that will be worthwhile forever. He will!

References

Chapter 1: Introduction

1. See, for example, other lines of evidence sketched in the following works: Josh McDowell, *Evidence That Demands a Verdict* (Campus Crusade, 1972); Alan Hayward, *God Is* (Nelson, 1980); C. S. Lewis, *Mere Christianity* (Macmillan, 1952); S. I. McMillen and David E. Stern, *None of These Diseases*, 2nd ed. (Revell, 1984); Gary Habermas and Antony Flew, *Did Jesus Rise from the Dead?* (Harper and Row, 1987); and John L. Wiester, *The Genesis Connection* (Nelson, 1983).

Chapter 2: Biblical Prophecy and Pagan Oracles

1. Naturally, some deny the historicity of either or both the Hebrew and Greek accounts. See, e.g., Robert H. Pfeiffer, *Introduction to the Old Testament* (New York: Harper and Brothers, 1941); Joseph Fontenrose, *The Delphic Oracle* (Berkeley: University of California Press, 1978).
2. A complete catalog of the surviving Delphic responses is found in Fontenrose, *Delphic Oracle*; also H. W. Parke and D. E. W. Wormell, *The Delphic Oracle II: The Oracular Responses* (Oxford: Blackwell, 1956).
3. John Potter, *The Antiquities of Greece* (2 vols., 1697-98), book 2, chs 7-12; more accessible are the relevant articles in M. Cary, A. D. Nock, *et al*, eds. *The Oxford Classical Dictionary* (Oxford: Clarendon Press, 1949), and Sir William Smith, William Wayte and G. E. Marindin, *Dictionary of Greek and Roman Antiquities* (3rd ed.; London: John Murray, 1890-91; frequently reprinted).
4. Diodorus Siculus, *Library of History* 16.26.2.
5. Pausanius, *Description of Greece* 9.39.5.
6. Ibid., 9.39.7-8.
7. Ibid., 9.39.10-11.
8. Potter, *Antiquities*, book 2, ch 9.
9. Herodotus, *History* 1.50-51.
10. Cicero, *De Divinatione* 2.56 (115-16).
11. Herodotus, *History* 1.91.
12. Ibid., 1.66.
13. Ibid., 1.67-68.
14. Ibid., 7.140-142.
15. Plutarch, *Life of Themistocles* 10.1
16. Plutarch, *Life of Demosthenes* 20.

Chapter 3: The Destruction of Tyre

1. J. B. Pritchard, *Ancient Near Eastern Texts* (Princeton: Princeton University Press, 1955). See especially the use of the phrase "in the midst of the sea," which is applied to both Tyre and Sidon, though the latter has no insular development, p 291. This phrase cannot, therefore, refer to insular Tyre. Nor do the remarks of Ezekiel 26 fit an island city, as we shall see. Rather the onshore city is in view.
2. Josephus, *Against Apion* 1.21.
3. The introductions to the Loeb Classical Library editions of Diodorus, Curtius and Arrian (London: William Heinemann, and Cambridge: Harvard University Press) contain excellent analyses of the historical sources and perspectives of each of these ancient writers.
4. Arrian, *History of Alexander and Indica* 2.18.
5. Curtius, *History of Alexander* 4.2.8.
6. Diodorus, *Library of History* 17.40.1-3.
7. Curtius, 4.2.18.
8. Diodorus, *loc. cit.*; Curtius reports six thousand, Arrian eight thousand.
9. Arrian, 2.18, reports thirty thousand.

10. Arrian, 2.18.

11. Diodorus, 9.57.58.

12. R. H. Pfeiffer, *Introduction to the Old Testament* (New York: Harper and Brothers, 1941), p 525.

13. Robert Dick Wilson, *A Scientific Investigation of the Old Testament* (Chicago: Moody Press, 1959 reprint), p 99.

14. Pfeiffer, *Introduction*, p 526.

15. H. G. May and E. L. Allen, *The Interpreter's Bible*, 6:42.

16. Pfeiffer, *Introduction*, p 525.

17. *Interpreter's Bible*, 6:45.

18. Ibid., p 51.

19. See C. C. Torrey, *Pseudo-Ezekiel and the Original Prophecy*; and Pfeiffer, *Introduction*, p 523.

20. Shalom Spiegel, *Harvard Theological Review* 24 (1931), 291.

21. Ibid., p 317.

22. Pfeiffer, *Introduction*, p 531.

23. G. A. Cooke, *The Book of Ezekiel* (New York: Charles Scribners Sons, 1937), p xxiv.

24. W. Eichrodt, *Ezekiel, a Commentary* (Philadelphia: Westminster Press, 1970), p 368.

25. R. K. Harrison, *Introduction to the Old Testament* (Grand Rapids: Eerdmans, 1969), pp 522-55.

26. Torrey (see note 19, above) is a prime example of one holding such an interpretation.

27. G. C. Oxtoby, *Prediction and Fulfillment in the Bible* (Philadelphia: Westminster Press, 1966), p 79.

Chapter 4: Alexander's Conquest of Palestine

1. Hobart Freeman, *An Introduction to the Old Testament Prophets* (Chicago: Moody Press, 1968), pp 340-42. Freeman answers Mede's criticisms.

2. Recent proponents of a pre-exilic date include Norman K. Gottwald, *All the Kingdoms of the Earth* (New York: Harper and Row, 1964); E. G. Kraeling, "The Historical Situation in Zech 9:1-10," *American Journal of Semitic Languages and Literatures* 41 (1924), 24-33; and A. Malamat, "The Historical Setting of Two Biblical Prophecies on the Nations," *Israel Exploration Journal* 1 (1950-51), 149-54. These argue that chapter 9 alludes to the Assyrian campaigns of 739-720 BC.

3. J. S. Wright, "Zechariah, Book of" in *The New Bible Dictionary*, ed. J. D. Young (Grand Rapids: Eerdmans, 1962), p 354.

4. R. K. Harrison, *Introduction to the Old Testament* (Grand Rapids: Eerdmans, 1969), p 953.

5. G. E. Ladd, "Apocalyptic" in *The New Bible Dictionary*, pp 43-44; and "Why Not Prophetic-Apocalyptic?" *Journal of Biblical Literature* 72 (1957), 192-200.

6. John Bright, "Faith and Destiny," *Interpretation* 5 (1951), 4-24. The prophetic-apocalyptic element is particularly strong in Amos and the so-called "Second Isaiah." Both are considered to come from several centuries before the Maccabean period.

7. E. B. Pusey, *The Minor Prophets* (New York: Funk and Wagnalls, 1885), p 327; and Joyce Baldwin, *Haggai, Zechariah, Malachi* (Downers Grove, IL: InterVarsity, 1972), pp 70-81.

8. D. Barthelmy, *Les Devanciers d'Aquila* (Leiden: E. J. Brill, 1963), pp 170-78.

9. P. Lamarche, *Zacharie IX-XIV* (Paris: Gabalda, 1961).

10. Baldwin, *Haggai, Zechariah, Malachi*, p 77. That a connection exists between the shepherd and king passages is seen in Ezek 34:23-24.

11. The Greek Septuagint translation of the OT translates *b'eretz* by *en ge*.

12. Josephus, *Antiquities* 11.7.13.

13. James Pritchard, *Ancient Near Eastern Texts Relating to the Old Testament*, 2nd ed.

(Princeton: Princeton University Press, 1955), pp 282-83.

14. e.g., C. Keil, *The Twelve Minor Prophets*, 2 vols. (Grand Rapids: Eerdmans, 1951 reprint), 2:332.

15. Douglas R. Jones, "A Fresh interpretation of Zechariah IX-XI," *Vetus Testamentum* 12 (1962), 244.

16. A lively account is also given in J. B. Bury, S. A. Cook and F. E. Adcock, eds., *The Cambridge Ancient History* (Cambridge: Cambridge University Press, 1965), 6:374-76.

17. David Baron, *The Visions and Prophecies of Zechariah* (Grand Rapids: Kregel, 1972 reprint), p 272.

18. Arrian, *History of Alexander and Indica* 2.17.2.

19. Ibid., 2.17.5.

20. Curtius, *History of Alexander* 4.4.13.

21. A. T. Olmstead, *History of the Persian Empire* (Chicago: University of Chicago Press, 1948), pp 507-08. Ancient sources are Arrian, 2.26-27; and Curtius, 4.6.7-29.

22. Josephus, *Antiquities* 14.5.3; *War* 1.8.4. A mixed population is implied.

23. W. L. Alexander, *Zechariah: His Visions and Warnings* (Toronto: S. R. Briggs, 1885), pp 158-59.

24. e.g., Baron, *Visions and Prophecies*, pp 299-302; Pusey, *Minor Prophets*, pp 400-01; Merrill F. Unger, *Zechariah* (Grand Rapids: Zondervan, 1963), p 157.

25. Josephus, *Antiquities* 11.8.3

26. Arrian, 3.1.1.

27. Curtius, 4.2.7.

28. William F. Albright, as quoted in Joseph P. Free, *Archaeology and Bible History* (Wheaton: Van Kampen, 1950), pp 264-65.

29. Pusey, *Minor Prophets*, pp 400-01.

Chapter 5: The Fall of Nineveh

1. Some other methods, besides (1) post-dating the prophecy, are: (2) intentional fulfillment; (3) coincidence; (4) alleging vagueness; (5) extra-sensory perception.

2. Robert H. Pfeiffer, *Introduction to the Old Testament* (New York: Harper and Brothers, 1941), pp 594-95.

3. Ibid.

4. A very thorough treatment of the acrostic problem may be found in Walter A. Maier, *The Book of Nahum: A Commentary* (St. Louis: Concordia, 1959).

5. Ibid., p 69.

6. Ibid., pp 69-70.

7. *The Inscriptions of Ashurbanipal*, column 2, lines as indicated; cited in George Smith, *Assyrian Discoveries* (New York: Scribner, Armstrong and Co., 1876), pp 328-29.

8. James H. Breastead, *The History of Egypt* (New York: Charles Scribner's Sons, 1905), pp 567-68.

9. Maier, *Nahum*, pp 38-39.

10. J. M. P. Smith, W. H. Ward and J. A. Bewer, *A Critical and Exegetical Commentary on Micah, Zephaniah, Nahum, Habakkuk, Obadiah and Joel* in *The International Critical Commentary* (New York: Charles Scribner's Sons, 1911), p 278. Recent archeological investigations have turned up scrolls of the Minor Prophets, both in the original Hebrew and in Greek translation, which were copied before the time of Christ.

11. R. K. Harrison, *Introduction to the Old Testament* (Grand Rapids: Eerdmans, 1969), pp 926-30.

12. Smith, Ward and Bewer, *International Critical Commentary*, p 275.

13. Pfeiffer, *Introduction*, pp 596-97.

14. Breastead, *History of Egypt*, pp 567-68.

15. Herodotus, *History* 1.102-06. Apparently Herodotus (section 106) intended to

write a history specifically of Assyria. If he did, no such work has survived.

16. Smith, Ward and Bewer, *International Critical Commentary*, pp 275-76.
17. *Inscriptions of Ashurbanipal*, column 5, in Smith, *Assyrian Discoveries*, pp 343-46.
18. Sir Austen Henry Layard, *Popular Account of Discoveries at Nineveh* (1857), p 321, quoted in Maier, *Nahum*, pp 125-26.
19. Maier, *Nahum*, p 126.
20. Diodorus Siculus, *Library of History* 2.26-27.
21. *The Babylonian Chronicle*, in D. Winton Thomas, ed., *Documents from Old Testament Times* (New York: Harper and Row, 1958), pp 75-76.
22. J. B. Bury, S. A. Cook and F. E. Adcock, eds., *The Cambridge Ancient History* (Cambridge: Cambridge University Press, 1965), 3:130.

Chapter 6: The Dispersion and Oppression of the Jews

1. See S. H. Kellogg, *The Jews; or, Prediction and Fulfillment* 2nd ed. (New York: Anson Randolph, 1887), chap 4.
2. Archibald Alexander Hodge, *Outlines of Theology*, rev ed. (New York: Robert Carter and Brothers, 1879), p 30.
3. William F. Albright, *Yahweh and the Gods of Canaan* (Garden City: Doubleday, 1968); Elmer B. Smick, "Israel's Struggle with the Religions of Canaan" in *Interpretation and History: Essays in Honour of Allan A. MacRae*, ed. R. Laird Harris, Swee-Hwa Quek and J. Robert Vannoy (Singapore: Christian Life Publishers, 1986), pp 123-133.
4. At most, the conclusions of the most radical critics would reduce the time of writing from 4000 years ago to 2500. But history written 2500 years in advance is still prediction, as much beyond human power and knowledge as the other. The apparently miraculous fact of foreknowledge, and of the prediction based upon it, which radical criticism is so anxious to be rid of, remains a stubborn fact.
5. See, e.g., William Henry Green, *The Higher Criticism of the Pentateuch* (New York: Scribners, 1895; reprint Grand Rapids: Baker, 1978), pp 150-156; Oswald T. Allis, *The Five Books of Moses* (Philadelphia: Presbyterian and Reformed, 1949), pp 201-202; Gleason L. Archer, Jr., *A Survey of Old Testament Introduction* (Chicago: Moody, 1964), chap 11.
6. We shall consider prophecies concerning the Messiah in Chapters 9-11.
7. Josephus, *Antiquities* 12.5.3.
8. Josephus, *War*, books 5 and 6.
9. "The Romans, weary of the work of slaughter, spared the people, but sold all the rest as slaves, though they bore but a low price, the market being glutted and few purchasers found; the number sold as slaves was incalculable." Henry H. Milman, *The History of the Jews* (New York: A. C. Armstrong & Son, 1880), 2:382.
10. Dio Cassius, *Roman History* 69.14.1.
11. "Jerusalem might almost seem to be a place under a peculiar curse; it has probably witnessed a greater portion of human misery than any other spot under the sun." Milman, *History of the Jews*, 2:385.
12. Edward Gibbon, *The History of the Decline and Fall of the Roman Empire* (1776-88), 5:554.
13. Jacques Basnage, *History of the Jews* (London: 1708), chap 28, sect 15.
14. Statistics on the holocaust may be found in *Encyclopaedia Judaica*, s.v. "Holocaust," 8:885-890.
15. Theodore Christlieb, *Modern Doubt and Christian Belief* (New York: Scribner, Armstrong & Co., 1874), p 333.

Chapter 7: Hosea's Prophetic History of the Jews

1. *The Zondervan Pictorial Encyclopedia of the Bible* (1976), s.v. "Hosea," by R. K. Harrison.
2. Robert H. Pfeiffer, *Introduction to the Old Testament* (New York: Harper and

Bros., 1941), p 567.

3. R. E. Clements, "Understanding the Book of Hosea," *Review and Expositor* 72 (1975): 412.

4. Ibid., p 417.

5. Robert Gordis, *Poets, Prophets, and Sages: Essays in Biblical Interpretation* (Bloomington: Indiana Univ. Press, 1971), p 253.

6. Ibid., p 245.

7. F. I. Anderson and D. N. Freedman, *Hosea*, in *The Anchor Bible* (Garden City: Doubleday, 1980), p 307.

8. Ibid., p 291. Note that the *Anchor Bible* wording of this clause produces a better parallelism of Hosea's marriage with the predicted fulfillment.

9. *Theological Wordbook of the Old Testament* (1980), s.v. *"reach"* by R. Laird Harris, 2:853.

10. T. K. Cheyne, *Hosea*, in *The Cambridge Bible for Schools and Colleges* (Cambridge: Cambridge Univ. Press, 1892), p 58.

11. H. H. Rowley, "The Marriage of Hosea," *Bulletin of the John Rylands Library* 39 (1956): 219.

12. Ibid., p 224.

13. Anderson and Freedman, *Hosea*, p 298.

14. W. P. Harper, *A Critical and Exegetical Commentary on Amos and Hosea*, in *The International Critical Commentary* (Edinburgh: T. and T. Clark, 1905), p 219.

15. H. S. Nyberg, *Studien zum Hoseabuch* (Uppsala: Almqvist und Wiksells, 1935), p 23.

16. Gordis, *Poets, Prophets, and Sages*, p 232.

17. Nyberg, *Hoseabuch*.

18. *Theological Wordbook of the Old Testament*, s.v. *"sar"*, by G. C. Cohen.

19. Harper, *Hosea*, p 221.

20. Jack Finegan, *Light from the Ancient Past* (Princeton: Princeton Univ. Press, 1959), 1:67.

21. Some doubt the rebelliousness of this succession since it was prophesied (1 Kings 11:29-39) and therefore in some sense in the will of God. However, God considered Jeroboam's actions to be rebellious because he did not obey the conditional promises of the prophecy (1 Kings 11:38) but instead built shrines in Bethel and Dan (1 Kings 12:26-33; 14:7-16). By the time of Hosea, the Northern Kingdom's kingship has been corrupted to the point that God says, "They have set up kings, but not by Me; they have appointed princes, but I did not know it" (Hos 8:4).

22. The Septuagint translates the "without list" as "king, prince, sacrifice, altar, priesthood and manifestations" (presumably *Urim and Thummim*), which is more indicative of the proper state than of the rebellious one.

23. The list in the Septuagint is constructed of genuine Mosaic elements, so that it predicts the abandonment of true worship, to which Israel will return in the last days. Such a rendering, however, must gloss over several clearly pagan terms (see "teraphim," above).

24. H. H. Ben-Sasson, ed., *A History of the Jewish People* (London: Weidenfeld and Nicolson, 1976), p 135.

25. James B. Pritchard, ed., *Ancient Near Eastern Texts Relating to the Old Testament*, 2nd ed. (Princeton: Princeton Univ. Press, 1955), p 284.

26. Ibid.

27. Ibid., pp 284-85.

28. Ben-Sasson, *History*, p 137.

29. H. L. Ellison, *Ezekiel: The Man and His Message* (Grand Rapids: Eerdmans, 1956), p 132.

30. Ben-Sasson, *History*, pp 137-38.

31. To gain an impression of the frequency of occurrence of the remnant concept in Scripture, consult an exhaustive concordance under the term "remnant", e.g., R. L.

Thomas, ed., *New American Standard Exhaustive Concordance of the Bible* (Nashville: Holman, 1981).

32. *Encyclopaedia Judaica* (1971), s.v. "Samaritans," by Benyamin Tsedaka.

33. *Zondervan Pictorial Encyclopedia of the Bible*, s.v. "Samaritans," by J. L. Kelso.

34. The following summary is paraphrased and condensed from articles on the Samaritans in *Encyclopaedia Britannica* (1970) by Theodore H. Gaster and in the two encyclopedias of notes 32 and 33.

35. The following discussion is condensed from Ben-Sasson, *History*, pp 303-13, 332-34.

36. John Urquhart, *The Wonders of Prophecy*, 9th ed. (Harrisburg: Christian Publications, n.d.), pp 236-37; Urquhart's discussion is closely paralleled by Ben-Sasson, *History*, pp 309-12.

37. Ben-Sasson, *History*, p 421.

38. Ibid., p 428.

39. Ibid., p 432.

40. Ibid., pp 811, 849.

41. J. Barton Payne, *Encyclopedia of Biblical Prophecy* (New York: Harper and Row, 1973), p 111.

42. H. H. Milman, *The History of the Jews*, 5th ed. (London: John Murray, 1883), 2:414.

43. *Encyclopaedia Judaica*, s.v. "History," by Michael Avi-Yonah.

44. David Kimchi, quoted without citation in E. Henderson, *The Twelve Minor Prophets* (1858; reprt. Grand Rapids: Baker, 1980), pp 17-18.

45. 1 Sam 2:27-36 and 3:11-14. This prophecy began to be fulfilled with the death of Eli's sons (1 Sam 4:11), continued with the murder of the priests of Nob (1 Sam 22:6-19), and was completed with the Abiathar's dismissal from the high priesthood (1 Kings 2:27). The fulfilment thus occurred in stages taking over a century to complete.

46. Kimchi, quoted without citation in Henderson *Twelve Minor Prophets*, p 19. For a nearly complete collection of rabbinical references to the Messiah, see Louis Ginzberg, *The Legends of the Jews* (Philadelphia: Jewish Publication Society, 1913-38), 6:272 n128; Alfred Edersheim, *The Life and Times of Jesus the Messiah* 3rd ed. (1886; reprt. Grand Rapids: Eerdmans, 1967), 2:710-41.

Chapter 8: The Return of the Jews

1. Samuel H. Kellogg, whose work was employed in chapter 6, represents such a literal interpreter. See his entire work, cited in footnote 1 of that chapter.

2. A. Berkeley Mickelsen, *Interpreting the Bible* (Grand Rapids: Eerdmans, 1963), p 289.

3. Ibid.; J. Robert Vannoy, lecture notes on the Old Testament prophets, Biblical Theological Seminary, 1974.

4. Bernard Ramm, *Protestant Biblical Interpretation* (Grand Rapids: Baker, 1970), p 249.

5. Mickelsen, *Interpreting the Bible*, p 296.

6. Allan A. MacRae, lecture notes on Isaiah, Biblical Theological Seminary, 1974; see also his *Gospel of Isaiah* (Chicago: Moody, 1977), chap 4.

7. Francis Brown, S. R. Driver and Charles A. Briggs, *A Hebrew and English Lexicon of the Old Testament* (Oxford: Clarendon Press, 1904), p 651.

8. Ibid., p 629.

9. Ibid., p 888-89; see also Alexander Harkavy, *Students' Hebrew and Chaldee Dictionary of the Old Testament* (New York: Hebrew Publishing Co., 1914), pp 663-64.

10. George Buchanan Gray, *A Critical and Exegetical Commentary on the Book of Isaiah* (Edinburgh: T. & T. Clark, 1912), 1:226.

11. Otto Kaiser, *Isaiah 1-12: A Commentary* (Philadelphia: Westminster Press, 1972), p 164.

12. *Encyclopaedia Judaica* (1972), 13:869. Population estimates are very uncertain.

13. Josephus, *Antiquities* 9.14.1.

14. *Encyclopaedia Judaica*, 6:1040.

15. Detailed maps of the exile and return of Israel may be found in Yohanan Aharoni and Michael Avi-Yonah, *The Macmillan Bible Atlas* (New York: Macmillan, 1968), maps 96, 105, 108.

16. Efraim Orni and Elisha Efrat, *Geography of Israel*, 3rd rev. ed. (Jerusalem: Israel Universities press, 1973), pp 214-15.

17. Ibid., pp 217-19.

18. Ibid., pp 219-21.

19. Ibid., pp 221-22.

20. Ibid., pp 222-23.

21. Ibid., pp 223-26.

22. Ibid., pp 227-51.

23. *Encyclopaedia Judaica*, 5:1502.

24. Ibid., 6:501.

25. Ibid., 6:497-501.

26. Ibid., 8:1449; 13:896.

27. Ibid., 8:1453.

28. Ibid., 15:646.

29. Ibid., 8:1439, 1441.

30. Personal correspondence, December 12, 1983, from Oded Ben-Haim, Consulate General of Israel, Philadelphia.

31. See the data on population distribution in *Encyclopaedia Judaica*, 13:889-896.

32. See J. Barton Payne, *Encyclopedia of Biblical Prophecy* (New York: Harper and Row, 1973), for a careful attempt to categorize all Biblical predictions by particular eras of past or future fulfillment. Hal Lindsey, *Late, Great Planet Earth* (Grand Rapids: Zondervan, 1970) is the most popular of many attempts to picture what the events of the end of the age will look like if they happen in this generation. Particular predictions relating to the Jews in the end-times are given in Isaiah 24-27, Ezekiel 36-48, Daniel 7, 9, 11-12, Zechariah 12-14, and parts of Revelation 7-22, as well as numerous scattered passages.

Chapter 9: The Person of the Messiah

1. English translations of most of these works are found in R. H. Charles, ed., *The Apocrypha and Pseudepigrapha of the Old Testament*, 2 vols. (Oxford: Clarendon Press, 1910) and in James H. Charlesworth, ed., *The Old Testament Pseudepigrapha*, 2 vols. (Garden City: Doubleday, 1983-85).

2. Among many discussions of the Dead Sea scrolls, see F. M. Cross, Jr., *The Ancient Library of Qumran and Modern Biblical Studies*, 2nd ed. (Garden City: Doubleday, 1961); William S. LaSor, *The Dead Sea Scrolls and the New Testament* (Grand Rapids: Eerdmans, 1972); and G. Vermes, *The Dead Sea Scrolls in English* (Baltimore: Penguin, 1968). Vermes also gives translations of the writings peculiar to the Qumran sect.

3. The standard English translation is Isidore Epstein, ed., *The Babylonian Talmud*, 35 vols. (London: Soncino, 1935-52). For aid in exploring this vast collection, I suggest Hermann L. Strack, *Introduction to Talmud and Midrash* (New York: Atheneum, 1969 reprint) and A. Cohen, *Everyman's Talmud* (New York: Schocken, 1978 reprint).

4. A convenient discussion of O.T. passages understood by the rabbis as prophetic of the Messiah is provided by Alfred Edersheim, *The Life and Times of Jesus the Messiah*, 2 vols., 3rd ed. (Grand Rapids: Eerdmans, 1967 reprint), 2: appendix IX.

5. *Manual of Discipline* 9.10.

6. See the discussion in Millar Burrows, *More Light on the Dead Sea Scrolls* (New York: Viking, 1958), pp 297-99; and in Vermes, *DSS in English*, pp 48-49.

7. T. Levi 18:16.

8. T. Judah 24:9.

9. Edersheim, *Life and Times*, 2:720-21; note also Jesus' remark to the Pharisees in Matt 23:41-46.

10. See the discussion in Edersheim, *Life and Times*, 2:710-737. Especially significant are Psalm 45, Isaiah 9 and Daniel 7.

11. For Psalm 22, see Edersheim, *Life and Times*, 2:718; for Isaiah 53, ibid., p 727; for Zechariah 12, ibid., p 736.

12. *Babylonian Talmud*, Sanhedrin 98b.

13. See the *Jewish Encyclopedia*, 8:511-512; *Encyclopaedia Judaica*, 11:1411.

14. *Babylonian Talmud*, Sukkah 52a.

15. For references to this glory of God, see, e.g., Ex 13:21; 14:19ff; 20:21-22; 1 Kings 8:10-13; Ezk 1; 10; 11:22-23; 43:1-7.

16. *Babylonian Talmud*, Sanhedrin 98a.

17. Ibid.

18. e.g., 4 Ezra 7:29.

19. *Babylonian Talmud*, Hagiga 14a.

20. Assumption of Moses 10:1-3.

21. 1 Enoch 46:1.

22. *Babylonian Talmud*, Sanhedrin 98a.

23. 4 Ezra 12:32.

24. The Jewish Publication Society's *Holy Scriptures According to the Masoretic Text* (1917, 1945) only transliterates the titles in the text, relegating the translation to a footnote where it is handled as a sentence referring to God *rather than* to the Messiah: "Wonderful in counsel is God the Mighty, the everlasting Father, the Ruler of peace." The *New English Bible* (1970) translates the phrase *'el gibbor* here as "in battle God-like," though elsewhere in that translation it is always rendered "God Almighty"!

Chapter 10: The Time of the Messiah

1. Suetonius, *The Lives of the Caesars*, "The Deified Vespasian," 4.5.

2. Tacitus, *Histories*, 5.13.

3. Josephus, *Jewish War*, 6.5.4.

4. See, for example, Jack Finegan, *Light from the Ancient Past*, 2nd ed. (Princeton: Princeton University Press, 1959), p 330.

5. *Babylonian Talmud*, Sanhedrin 97b.

6. Some of the earliest Christian commentators: Clement of Alexandria (c 200 AD), *Miscellanies*, 1.21; Tertullian (c 200), *An Answer to the Jews*, 8; Origen (c 225), *De Principiis*, 4.1.5.

7. See several alternatives in J. Barton Payne, *Encyclopedia of Biblical Prophecy* (New York: Harper and Row, 1973), pp 383-389.

8. Sir Robert Anderson, *The Coming Prince*, 10th ed. (London: James Nisbet, 1915; reprint Grand Rapids: Kregel, 1957).

9. Ibid., pp v-vi.

10. Ibid., p 72.

11. Ibid., p 122.

12. Jack Finegan, *Handbook of Biblical Chronology* (Princeton: Princeton University Press, 1964), sections 58-61.

13. Ibid., sections 454-468.

14. A revision of Robert C. Newman, "Daniel's Seventy Weeks and the Old Testament Sabbath-Year Cycle," *Journal of the Evangelical Theological Society* 16 (1973): 229-234.

15. Incidentally, a remark by the rabbis also associates the coming of the Messiah with a seven-year period. *Babylonian Talmud*, Sanhedrin 97a.

16. As also the King James Version, the Berkeley Version, the Amplified Bible, the Living Bible, the American Standard Version and the Jerusalem Bible.

17. Including the Jewish Publication Society's translation, the New English Bible, the

Smith-Goodspeed and Moffatt translations, and the New American Bible.

18. See, for example, K. Elliger and W. Rudolph, *Biblica Hebraica Stuttgartensia*, editio minor (Stuttgart: Deutsche Bibelgesellschaft, 1984), p 1404.

19. Ernst Wurtwein, *The Text of the Old Testament* (Oxford: Basil Blackwell, 1957), p 19

20. As suggested in the Berkeley Version. Smith-Goodspeed and the New English Bible imply such an interpretation by translating verse 25b: "for sixty-two weeks it shall *stay* rebuilt/ *remain* restored," but these translations of the verb *shub* find no warrant in the lexicons and merely show the problem of adopting the Masoretic punctuation.

21. See Payne, *Encyclopedia of Biblical Prophecy*, pp 383-386.

22. Finegan, *Biblical Chronology*, section 336.

23. Ibid., sections 194-195.

24. *Encyclopaedia Judaica*, 14:585.

25. Benedict Zuckermann, "Ueber Sabbatjahrcyclus und Jobelperiode," *Jahresbericht des juedisch-theologischen Seminars Fraenckelscher Stiftung* (Breslau, 1857).

26. Ben Zion Wacholder, "The Calendar of Sabbatical Cycles During the Second Temple and the Early Rabbinic Period," *Hebrew Union College Annual* 44 (1973): 153-196.

27. Ibid., pp 156, 163.

28. A complete table from 519 BC to AD 441 is given at the end of Wacholder's article, ibid., pp 185-196.

29. The sabbatical year seems to have started in the fall, Lev 25:8-10.

Chapter 11: The Work of the Messiah

1. An excellent examination of the servant passages of Isaiah is Allan A. MacRae, *The Gospel of Isaiah* (Chicago: Moody Press, 1977).

2. We have used the NIV here instead of Aston's own translation, as he makes several conjectural emendations of the Hebrew text. While there are probably a number of places in the Hebrew Bible which do not preserve the original text, the emendation of prophetic passages to give a better fit with the fulfilment is very much like begging the question. We have, in verse 9, opted for a translation suggested by MacRae, *Gospel of Isaiah*, pp 140-144, as more accurately representing what the Hebrew really says than does the NIV.

3. Verses indicated for each item are numbered, and the strophes of each verse are lettered (a, b, c, etc.) in the order given in the translation above. The chapter is 53 unless otherwise noted.

4. Bernhard Duhm, *Das Buch Jesaja* 4th ed. (Goettingen, 1922), p 393.

5. George Adam Smith, *The Book of Isaiah*, rev. ed. (London, 1927), 2:375.

6. Hugo Gressman, *Der Messias* (Goettingen, 1929), p 307.

7. August Wuensche, *Die Leiden des Messias* (Leipzig, 1870). See especially *Babylonian Talmud*, Sanhedrin 93a, 98b.

8. Emil Schuerer, *Geschichte des juedischen Volkes im Zeitalter Jesu Christi*, 4th ed. (Leipzig, 1907), 2:650.

9. See Samson H. Levey, *The Messiah: An Aramaic Interpretation* (Cincinnati: Hebrew Union College - Jewish Institute of Religion, 1974), pp 63-67, for a translation and discussion of this paraphrase.

10. S. R. Driver and Adolf Neubauer, *The Fifty-Third Chapter of Isaiah according to the Jewish Interpreters* (Oxford, 1877), p 337.

11. Quoted in Raymundus Marti, *Pugio Fidei* (Leipzig, 1687 reprint), p 416. Marti's work, originally published c 1278, included many compilations from old rabbinic manuscripts in which Isaiah 53 is applied to the Messiah.

12. *Pesikta Rabbati*, 37; quoted in *Yalkut Shimoni* on Isa 60, sect 499.

13. David Levy, *Prayers for the Day of Atonement*, 2nd ed. (London, 1807), 3:37.

14. Lebanon symbolizes the Mount of the Temple, where the Messiah is to appear.

15. Yinnon is a Talmudic term for the Messiah in His pre-existent life, as the Talmud renders Ps 72:17: "Before the sun [was created], Yinnon was His name." *Babylonian Talmud*, Sanhedrin 98b.

16. Driver and Neubauer, *53rd Chapter*, p 319.

17. Ibid., p 258.

Chapter 12: Conclusions

1. See a complete listing in J. Barton Payne, *Encyclopedia of Biblical Prophecy* (New York: Harper and Row, 1973).

Indices

Scripture Index

Subject Index